STUDENT UNIT GUIDE

NEW EDITION

AQA A2 Law Unit 4 (Sections A & B)

Criminal Law (Offences Against Property) and Law of Tort

Jennifer Currer, Jacqueline Hankins
and Ian Yule

PHILIP ALLAN

Philip Allan, an imprint of Hodder Education, an Hachette UK company, Market Place, Deddington, Oxfordshire OX15 0SE

Orders
Bookpoint Ltd, 130 Milton Park, Abingdon, Oxfordshire OX14 4SB
tel: 01235 827827
fax: 01235 400401
e-mail: education@bookpoint.co.uk
Lines are open 9.00 a.m.–5.00 p.m., Monday to Saturday, with a 24-hour message answering service.
You can also order through the Philip Allan website: www.philipallan.co.uk

© Jennifer Currer, Jacqueline Hankins and Ian Yule 2013

ISBN 978-1-4441-7209-6

First printed 2013
Impression number 5 4 3 2 1
Year 2016 2015 2014 2013

Cover photo: blas/Fotolia

AQA examination questions are reproduced by permission of the Assessment and Qualifications Alliance.

Typeset by Integra Software Services Pvt. Ltd., Pondicherry, India

Printed in Dubai

Hachette UK's policy is to use papers that are natural, renewable and recyclable products and made from wood grown in sustainable forests. The logging and manufacturing processes are expected to conform to the environmental regulations of the country of origin.

Contents

Content Guidance

Section A: Criminal law (offences against property) 6

Theft • Robbery • Burglary • Making off without payment • Criminal damage
Fraud • Blackmail • Duress • Intoxication • Self-defence/prevention of crime

Section B: Law of tort 28

Product liability • Medical negligence • Psychiatric injury
Economic loss • Occupiers' liability • Nuisance
The rule in *Rylands* v *Fletcher* • Vicarious liability
General defences • Remedies

Questions and Answers

Getting the most from this book

Questions & Answers

Questions & Answers

Question 3 Theft, fraud, obtaining services dishonestly and making off without payment

Uma and Violet were employed by Warren. One day at work, Uma discovered that Violet had left her purse in the toilets. Uma removed a fitness club membership card from the purse and then put the purse in the wastepaper bin (from which it was later removed and returned to Violet by an alert colleague). Uma subsequently used the membership card to get herself a training session at the fitness club, for which she would normally have had to pay £10. She quietly dropped the card at the reception desk when she left.

Adapted from AQA examination paper, January 2007

Discuss Uma's criminal liability for a range of property offences arising out of the incidents involving the purse and the use of the membership card. (25 marks)

As with all such scenario 'problem-solving' questions, you are required to identify relevant legal issues, define and explain relevant legal rules and then to apply these to provide (for a sound response) 'a sustainable analysis leading to satisfactory conclusions'. You need to use cases effectively to explain rules.

A-grade answer

Uma's criminal liability regarding the purse and membership card amounts to theft. Under s.1(1) of the Theft Act 1968: 'A person is guilty of theft if he dishonestly appropriates property belonging to another with the intention of permanently depriving the other of it.' In this scenario, Uma has appropriated the purse and card within the definition in s.3 of the Act because she has assumed 'the rights of an owner' over them. Both items are clearly tangible items and would be deemed as personal property under section 4, and both the card and purse did not belong to Uma. All the elements of the actus reus therefore seem to have been met.

The offence of theft is clearly defined and all elements of the actus reus are well applied using legal terminology.

Before Uma can be found guilty, it must be shown that she had the necessary mens rea, i.e. was dishonest in appropriating these items as, clearly, her actions do not fall within s.2's definitions of appropriations that are not to be regarded as dishonest. Applying the R v Ghosh test, what she did was dishonest, according to the ordinary standards of reasonable and honest people, and she must have realised that what she was doing was by those standards dishonest.

Her borrowing of the membership card brings her within the scope of s.6(1) of the Act: 'A person appropriating property belonging to another without meaning the other permanently to lose the thing itself is nevertheless to be regarded as having the intention of permanently depriving the other of it if his intention is to treat the thing

76

AQA A2 Law

Exam-style questions

Examiner comments on the questions

Tips on what you need to do to gain full marks, indicated by the icon e.

Sample student answers

Practise the questions, then look at the student answers that follow each set of questions.

Examiner commentary on sample student answers

Find out how many marks each answer would be awarded in the exam and then read the examiner comments (preceded by the icon e) following each student answer.

About this book

The AQA specification for the A2 Law examinations is divided into two units. This guide covers the two separate substantive law options in Unit 4 — Criminal Law (Offences against Property) and the Law of Tort. Property offences include theft, burglary, robbery, criminal damage, blackmail, fraud (sections 2 and 11 of the Fraud Act 2006) and making off without payment. Tort law includes the elements of the tort of negligence from Unit 3 and builds on these, covering nervous shock, pure economic loss, occupiers' liability, nuisance, vicarious liability and *Rylands v Fletcher*.

This is a substantive, 'real law' unit, which means that the examination is a 'problem-solving' paper that requires you to be able to use case law effectively.

The examination for this unit lasts 2 hours. It comprises two scenario-based questions on each topic, one of which must be selected. Each question consists of two parts, (a) and (b), which are both problem-solving questions. The final part of the examination paper deals with concepts of law and requires you to answer one question chosen from three.

There are two sections to this guide:
- **Content Guidance** — this sets out the specification content for Unit 4 (Sections A & B) and contains references to cases that you will need to study for a sound understanding of each topic.
- **Questions and Answers** — this section provides questions covering all topics, followed by A-grade answers, demonstrating how to employ case law to best effect and how to apply appropriate legal rules to answer the question set. Examiner comments explain the elements of the answers for which marks are awarded.

Content Guidance

Section A: Criminal law (offences against property)

Theft

Theft is a stand-alone offence as well as being an important part of the offences of robbery and burglary. A good understanding of this offence is, therefore, vital to your knowledge of other offences within this unit.

Theft is defined in s.1 of the **Theft Act 1968**, which states: 'A person is guilty of theft if he dishonestly appropriates property belonging to another with the intention of permanently depriving the other of it.' This definition can be split up into *actus reus* (guilty act) and *mens rea* (guilty mind), and both must be present if a defendant is to be found guilty. In answers to exam questions, each element should first be explained and then applied in turn, starting with the *actus reus*.

Actus reus

The *actus reus* of appropriating property belonging to another is defined in sections 3, 4 and 5 of the **Theft Act 1968**.

Section 3: appropriation

'Appropriates' is defined under s.3(1), which states: 'Any assumption by a person of the rights of an owner amounts to an appropriation.' This means that the defendant must have taken the item and treated it as his or her own. The rights of an owner can include:

- selling
- destroying
- hiring out
- lending

For example, if someone takes a book from a library and sells it, he or she will be deemed to have treated it as his or her own, and therefore found to have appropriated it. Only the owner has the right to sell the book. It is worth noting that appropriation does not take place until the owner's rights have been assumed. If Josh borrows a DVD from Jasbinder but innocently forgets to return it to him, he has not appropriated it. However, if Josh discovers the DVD and decides to sell it at a car-boot sale, it is at this point (the decision to sell) that he will be deemed to have 'appropriated' the DVD, and therefore treated it as his own.

> **Examiner tip**
>
> When applying appropriation to a scenario make sure you say how the item was appropriated and use correct legal definitions. For example: Fred appropriated the watch from George, he took it when he was not looking, he assumed the rights of the owner.

Rights

The case of *R* v *Morris* (1983) gave rise to the question whether 'rights' means 'all rights' or 'any rights'. The defendant had switched the price labels on items in a supermarket, giving lower prices to more expensive items. He then paid the lower prices. The courts had to determine whether, for 'assumption by a person of the rights of an owner' to be proved, the assumption had to be of *all* the rights or whether it could be of *any* of the rights. It was stated by the House of Lords that it was enough to prove 'the assumption...of *any* of the rights of the owner of the goods'.

Consent

Can a defendant be deemed to have appropriated an item when consent has been given by the owner? *R* v *Lawrence* (1971) clarified this situation, deciding that an item can be appropriated with the owner's consent. An Italian student, who spoke little English, hired a taxi, showing the driver the address to which he wanted to go. He offered the driver £1, but the driver indicated this was not enough, taking the £1 plus another £6 from the student's wallet. It was held by both the Court of Appeal and the House of Lords that this amounted to appropriation.

Knowledge check 1

Why can a defendant be deemed to have appropriated an item when consent has been given by the owner?

This point of law was backed up by *R* v *Gomez* (1993) and *R* v *Hinks* (2000). The courts commented that appropriation, if carried out with consent, must be looked at in conjunction with s.2 of the **Theft Act 1968**, defining 'dishonesty', so the question to ask was: did the defendant appropriate the item dishonestly? In *R* v *Hinks* the defendant was judged to have done just that, even though she had full consent from the owner, because the claimant was a vulnerable person who trusted her.

Section 4: property

Section 4(1) of the **Theft Act 1968** states that property 'includes money and all other property, real or personal, including things in action and other intangible property'. The definition clearly covers five types of property:
- **Money:** this includes all coins and banknotes of any currency.
- **Real property:** this means land and buildings, but under s.4(2) of the Theft Act 1968, the theft of land, or of things forming part of land, only arises:
  (a) where someone not in possession of the land appropriates something forming part of it by severing it or causing it to be severed, or after it has been severed, (for example, taking turf or a fixed concrete statue from someone else's garden)
  (b) where a tenant appropriates fixtures from the premises or land
- **Personal property:** this is tangible property (other than land and buildings) — items that can be seen, touched and moved and are not attached to the land. Examples are books, DVDs, watches and jewellery.
- **Things in action:** this refers to rights to recover money or personal property, which can be enforced against another person by an action in law. An example of this type of property is a bank account. If someone causes a debit to be made from someone else's bank account, this can be seen as appropriating a 'thing in action'.
- **Other intangible property:** this is property that cannot be touched. Examples include patents and export quotas.

Examiner tip

As with appropriation, you must make sure that you explain what type of property has been stolen. It is not sufficient to say it is just property — you must clarify what type of property. Also watch out for s.4(3) and s.4(4) — make sure the property being stolen is capable of being stolen, and if not explain why not.

Knowledge check 2

What point of law does *Oxford* v *Moss* give us?

Property that cannot be stolen

- In *Oxford* v *Moss* (1979), it was deemed that intangible property in the form of confidential information was not capable of being stolen, so the defendant, who had seen questions on an exam paper ahead of the actual exam, could not be held to have appropriated property.
- Section 4(3) of the **Theft Act 1968** states that picking fungi, flowers, foliage or fruit from the wild does not amount to theft, unless it is done for reward, sale or other commercial purpose.
- Section 4(4) of the **Theft Act 1968** states that wild creatures that are untamed or not ordinarily kept in captivity cannot be stolen unless they have been, or are being, 'reduced into possession' by someone else.

Section 5: belonging to another

Section 5(1) of the **Theft Act 1968** states: 'Property shall be regarded as belonging to any person having possession or control of it.' That person does not, therefore, necessarily have to be the legal owner of the property. For example, if David has hired a cement mixer for the day, he is not the legal owner (it remains the property of the hire company), but he is in possession and control of it. So if the mixer is taken from him without his permission, this will be seen as appropriating property 'belonging to another'.

Appropriating your own property

Following the case of *R* v *Turner (No. 2)* (1971), a person can be found guilty of appropriating property of which he or she is the legal owner. The defendant took his car to a garage to be repaired, having agreed to pay for the repairs when he collected the vehicle. The garage staff parked the car on the road outside their premises at the end of the day. During the night, the defendant used a spare key to remove the car without paying for the repairs. It was held by the Court of Appeal that the garage was in possession and control of the car and therefore the defendant could be found guilty of stealing what was his own property.

Property obtained by a mistake

Section 5(4) of the **Theft Act 1968** states:

> Where a person gets property by another's mistake, and is under an obligation to make restoration (in whole or in part) of the property or its proceeds or of the value thereof, then to the extent of that obligation the property or proceeds shall be regarded (as against him) as belonging to the person entitled to restoration, and an intention not to make restoration shall be regarded accordingly as an intention to deprive that person of the property or proceeds.

An example is where a shopper is given too much change. If the shopper fails to return the money, he or she could be liable under s.5(4), being deemed to have appropriated property that belonged to another. In *Attorney General's Reference (No. 1)* (1983), where an employer paid into an employee's bank account more salary than the employee was entitled to, the Court of Appeal held that the employee, having received the excess payment by her employer's mistake, was legally obliged to return it.

Knowledge check 3

A defendant is under an obligation to make restoration when he or she receives property by mistake. What is the leading case that gives us this point of law?

Examiner tip

When applying the *actus reus* to property offences explain and apply each element in turn. This gives a more structured, coherent answer. Remember to use the key definitions for each of the elements.

Mens rea

Section 2: dishonesty

The **Theft Act 1968** does not define the word 'dishonestly'. However, in s.2(1) it lists a number of situations where a person's appropriation of property belonging to another would *not* be classed as dishonest in the eyes of the law:

- Where the person believes that he or she has in law the right to deprive the other of the property. This might apply if the person believes the item concerned is in fact his or her own property.
- Where the person believes he or she would have the other person's consent if that other person knew of the appropriation. This might apply where a student borrows a flatmate's iPod in the honest belief that the flatmate would not mind.
- Where the person believes that the owner of the property cannot be traced by taking reasonable steps. This might apply where a person finds a £5 note, because he or she would probably be right in thinking that putting up a poster stating '£5 note found' would lead to a number of people claiming to be the owner, so that the real owner would be difficult to identify.

If none of the above situations fits the scenario, a two-stage test to determine dishonesty must be applied, following the court's ruling in *R v Ghosh* (1982). In that case, a doctor was found to have claimed fees for an operation that he had not carried out. Arguing that the same amount of money was legitimately payable to him for consultation fees, he said he had not been dishonest. After the jury members were directed to apply their own standards to decide if what he did was dishonest, he was convicted. Upon appeal, the court decided that the correct test should be based on both an objective and a subjective element.

Knowledge check 4

What are the three situations under s.2 of the Theft Act 1968 where the defendant would be deemed *not* to be dishonest?

Two-stage test from R v Ghosh

Two questions must be asked to determine whether the defendant has been dishonest:

(1) Was the action dishonest according to the standards of a 'reasonable and honest man'? This is an objective test, based on the opinion of a reasonable person in a given situation.

(2) Did the defendant realise that what he or she was doing was dishonest by those standards? This is a subjective test and it must be determined by trying to understand what the defendant was thinking at the time of the *actus reus*.

If the answer to both these questions is yes, then the defendant will be held to have been dishonest. If the answer to either of the questions is no, then the defendant will be held not to have been dishonest and therefore will not be guilty of the offence of theft under the **Theft Act 1968**.

Examiner tip

You must apply the *mens rea* in full to obtain full marks. It is not sufficient to say that the defendant was dishonest — you must say why he was dishonest and apply the R v *Ghosh* test in full.

Section 6: intention of permanently depriving the other

This is the final element that has to be proved if the defendant is to be found guilty of theft. Section 6(1) of the **Theft Act 1968** states:

> A person appropriating property belonging to another without meaning the other permanently to lose the thing itself is nevertheless to be regarded as having the

Examiner tip

Theft is a stand-alone offence as well as being a vital part of other offences under the Theft Act. Remember to follow the set rules when applying this offence: first define theft; then explain what the *actus reus* is and apply; finally explain the *mens rea* and then apply. Finish with a conclusion — is your defendant guilty or not?

intention of permanently depriving the other of it if his intention is to treat the thing as his own to dispose of regardless of the other's rights; and a borrowing or lending of it may amount to so treating it.

The defendant may have shown an intention to treat the thing as his or her own to dispose of by selling it, destroying it or spending it.

The Court of Appeal's decision in *R* v *Velumyl* (1989) shows that taking someone else's money, even with the honest intention of replacing it with an equivalent sum a couple of days later, can still amount to appropriating the money 'with the intention of permanently depriving the other of it'. The defendant in that case took £1,050 from his employer's safe to lend to a friend just for the weekend, intending to pay back money to the same value when the friend had repaid him. He was judged guilty of theft because he was not planning to replace the money with exactly the same notes or coins as he had taken.

Borrowing property

Under normal circumstances, there is no intention to permanently deprive when an item is borrowed because the intention is to return the object. However, the appeal court said in *R* v *Lloyd* (1985) that if the intention was to return the item in such a changed state that 'the goodness, the virtue and the practical value had gone out of the article', that would amount to an intention to permanently deprive for the purposes of s.6 of the **Theft Act 1968**. In that case, the defendant took films from a cinema, copied them and replaced them. This did not amount to theft, as the films' goodness and practical value were unchanged. However, if Greg takes Nikesh's ticket to a football match, watches the match and then returns the ticket, this clearly has an impact on the practical value of the ticket and shows intention to permanently deprive for the purposes of s.6.

Conditional intent

Knowledge check 5

Define the meaning of conditional intent.

Following *R* v *Easom* (1971), if a defendant's intention permanently to deprive is based on a condition, for example that something is actually worth stealing, that is not a sufficient intention for a conviction for theft. The defendant in that case picked up a woman's handbag in a cinema, looked inside and then replaced it without taking anything. He was not guilty of theft.

Summary

- **Appropriation.** The defendant must appropriate the property, assume the rights of the owner and treat it as his or her own (e.g. *R* v *Morris* — rights can be all or part; *R* v *Lawrence* — appropriation can be with the consent of the owner).

- **Property.** Property must be capable of being stolen: money, real property, personal property, things in action and other intangible property. Knowledge and information is not capable of being stolen (e.g. *Oxford* v *Moss*).

- **Belonging to another.** The property must belong to another — or the person who has possession and control of the property at the time of the theft (e.g. *R* v *Turner (No. 2)*).

- **Dishonesty.** The defendant must be dishonest as to the appropriation. *R* v *Ghosh* test is applied — would a reasonable person deem the actions of the defendant as dishonest, and did the defendant realise his actions were dishonest by those standards?

- **Intention to permanently deprive.** There must be an intent to permanently deprive. If something is taken it must be replaced with the exact same item (e.g. *R* v *Velumyl*). Conditional intent is not sufficient (e.g. *R* v *Easom*).

Robbery

The offence of robbery is defined in s.8(1) of the **Theft Act 1968**, which states:

> A person is guilty of robbery if he steals, and immediately before or at the time of doing
> so, and in order to do so, he uses force on any person or puts or seeks to put any person
> in fear of being then and there subjected to force.

Both *actus reus* and *mens rea* must be present if the defendant is to be found guilty.

Actus reus

The theft must be complete

For the defendant to be found guilty of robbery, the theft element of the crime must be complete. If any elements are missing, for example if the defendant did not have the intention to permanently deprive, or there is deemed to be no appropriation, there can be no offence of robbery. In *Corcoran* v *Anderton* (1980), the defendant hit a woman in the back while his accomplice pulled at her bag. The woman let go of the bag and it fell to the ground. The woman screamed, the defendant and his accomplice ran off and the woman was able to pick up her handbag. Even though neither the defendant nor his accomplice ever had sole control of the handbag, this was deemed to be a completed theft, the tugging at the handbag being sufficient exercise of control to be appropriation. As the tugging was force, and as it was at the time of the theft, the defendants were guilty of robbery. The theft would not have been complete if the woman had not let go of the bag, but there would have been an attempted theft, and as force was used, this would have amounted to attempted robbery.

Force or threat of force on the victim

If robbery is to be proved, the defendant must have used force or put the victim in fear of force. A threat of force is sufficient; actual physical force does not need to have been applied. An example would be where someone is threatened with being beaten up if he or she does not hand over a bag; this amounts to a threat of force. If the theft is then completed, the charge of robbery will be successful. Silence, as well as words, can constitute a threat, and so can the use of weapons.

The word 'force' is given its ordinary meaning by the courts. *R* v *Dawson and James* (1976) shows that force can be minimal: mere jostling or the slightest push. In this case, one of the defendants nudged the victim, who stumbled, and the other defendant then took the victim's wallet. The definition of 'force' can also be extended, as in *R* v *Clouden* (1987), where the Court of Appeal held that the force applied to a shopping basket when it was snatched from the victim amounted to indirect force.

The key is that the defendant must either put the victim in fear or seek to put the victim in fear, and it does not matter how this is achieved. It is important to remember that, as long as the defendant seeks to put the victim in fear, the offence is committed, whether or not the victim is actually frightened. Nor does the theft have to be from the person who is being threatened. It is still robbery if a man holds a bank customer

Knowledge check 6

In the case of *Corcoran* v *Anderton* the defendant did not successfully obtain the handbag. Why is this still deemed a completed theft?

Examiner tip

In any question involving robbery it is advisable that you first prove the theft. Explain and apply all elements of theft — *actus reus* and then *mens rea* — and then raise the charge to robbery. This will ensure that you have applied all elements.

Knowledge check 7

Which case shows that force can be minimal — mere jostling or the slightest push is sufficient?

at gunpoint while demanding money from the cashier, who hands the money over; the force is used against the customer, while the theft is from the bank.

Immediately before or at the time of the theft

A stipulation of this offence is that the force must occur either immediately before or at the time of the theft. If the force is separate in time from the theft, there is no robbery. For example, if two men are fighting and one is pushed to the ground unconscious, and the other then decides to take the injured man's wallet, this is not robbery. It is an offence against the person and theft — two separate crimes. Theft can, however, be regarded as a continuing act. In *R v Hale* (1978), the defendants had entered a house, and one of them tied up the occupant while the other went upstairs and took jewellery from the bedroom. The pair then left, leaving the victim tied up. Even though the jewellery may have been taken before force was applied to the victim, the Court of Appeal deemed this appropriation to be continuing, and therefore the force was seen to be 'at the time' of the stealing.

This can also be shown in the case of *Lockley*. The defendant entered a shop and clearly put cans of beer under his jacket, the shopkeeper saw this, and as the defendant was leaving, he tried to stop him. The defendant pushed him out the way. The push was deemed force, and it was deemed that the theft was a continuing act — the appropriation of the beer was continuing until he had left the shop, therefore the charge of robbery was successful.

Mens rea

For robbery to be proved, *mens rea* for theft must be present — the defendant must be dishonest (s.2 of the **Theft Act 1968**) in the appropriation, and must have the intention to permanently deprive the owner of the property (s.6). There must also be an intention to use force or a threat of force on the victim in order to steal.

Knowledge check 8

What important rule was laid down in *Hale* (1978) and upheld in *Lockley?*

Examiner tip

In the exam there are often questions that involve the various elements of robbery. Remember the key is to focus on the issues that require discussion. So look out for a continuing act and remember to raise the issue of when the theft is complete, citing *Hale* as your point of law.

Knowledge check 9

What is the *mens rea* for the offence of robbery?

Summary

Actus reus:

- **The theft must be complete.** All elements of theft must be proven. *Corcoran v Anderton* shows that the defendant does not have to successfully gain — as long as appropriation occurred at some point.

- **Force or threat of force on the victim.** There must be force or a threat of force. There is no requirement that the force be physical. It is also irrelevant that the victim may not actually be frightened. The meaning of force is down to the jury to decide, taking its ordinary meaning (e.g. *R v Dawson and James*). The force does not have to be directed at the victim.

- **Immediately before or at the time of the theft.** It is important when the force occurs — it must come either immediately before or at the time of the theft. Following *Hale* and *Lockley* the theft can be regarded as a continuing act and the force will be deemed to have been used at the time of the theft in these situations.

- **Mens rea:** the defendant must have full *mens rea* for the completed theft — he or she must be dishonest (s.2 **Theft Act 1968**) and must have the intention to permanently deprive the victim of the property (s.6). The defendant must also intend to use the force or threat of force to steal.

Burglary

Burglary is described in s.9 of the **Theft Act 1968**. There are two separate types of burglary, both of which involve the defendant trespassing onto premises. One type of burglary involves the defendant entering premises with the intent to commit one of three offences. The other type involves the defendant first trespassing onto the premises and then, once inside, committing one of two offences.

- **Section 9(1)(a)** The defendant enters a building or part of a building as a trespasser with the intent to commit any of three ulterior offences:
  - to steal
  - to inflict grievous bodily harm on any person in the building
  - to cause unlawful damage to the building or anything in it
- **Section 9(1)(b)** The defendant, having entered any building or part of a building as a trespasser, commits one of two offences:
  - stealing or attempting to steal
  - inflicting or attempting to inflict grievous bodily harm on any person in the building

Actus reus

Both types of burglary have similar elements, requiring a defendant to have entered a building or part of a building as a trespasser.

Entry

The definition of entry is not given in s.9, so the courts have relied on case law. *R* v *Collins* (1973) decided that entry has to be both 'substantial and effective', but in *R* v *Brown* (1985), it was held that entry had only to be effective. In *Brown*, the defendant was standing outside the building in question and leaned in through an open window to steal goods, which was deemed effective entry, although clearly not substantial. Then *R* v *Ryan* (1996) ruled that being stuck partway through a window, unable to reach anything to steal, was 'effective' entry.

Building or part of a building

The only definition of 'a building' for the purpose of burglary comes in s.9(4), which states that the term 'shall apply also to an inhabited vehicle or vessel, and shall apply...when the person having a habitation in it is not there as well as at times when he is'. The courts have helped to interpret the definition through case law, deciding that a building must have some permanence. So a shed that can easily be dismantled would appear not to be a building for the purpose of burglary. The more mobile the structure, the less likely it is to be classed as a building. In *Norfolk Constabulary* v *Seekings and Gould* (1986), the court held that a lorry trailer with wheels was not a building, even though it was not in working order as a trailer and had electricity connected. In *B and S* v *Leathley* (1979), a free-standing freezer container was held to be a building; it had stood in a farmyard for years, was no longer attached to a lorry and had electricity connected.

Examiner tip

Explain and apply the *mens rea* in full. If you prove theft first and then raise the charge to robbery you should have applied all the required elements. Make it clear, using evidence from the scenario, that the force or threat of force was used in order to steal — if this is not obvious then you must consider both outcomes, guilty or not guilty. Note that recklessness as to the use/threat of force is *not* part of the *mens rea*.

Knowledge check 10

What is the key difference between s.9(1)(a) and s.9(1)(b)?

Knowledge check 11

What is the definition of 'entry'?

Examiner tip

Always apply entry in full. It is not sufficient to say the defendant has entered the building — you must say how the defendant has entered the building.

Knowledge check 12

What point of law does the case of R v Walkington (1979) give us?

Examiner tip

It is important that you define building or part of a building before you apply the law. Remember — anything mobile would not be classed as a building.

Knowledge check 13

What is the definition of a trespasser?

Examiner tip

Always start your application of burglary by explaining what the *actus reus* is: entry, building or part of a building, as a trespasser. You can then apply and deal with the ulterior offences when you apply the *mens rea*.

Examiner tip

Remember this is offences against property — you are not expected to go into detail regarding any GBH.

Knowledge check 14

What is the *mens rea* needed to find a defendant guilty of burglary?

Examiner tip

When applying burglary it is always best to find the defendant guilty of the ulterior offence first. So if the defendant has stolen a DVD player from a house, first find him or her guilty for the theft of the DVD player and then raise the charge to burglary.

Use of the phrase 'part of a building' refers to situations where the defendant has permission to be in one part of a building but not in another. For example, the public has permission to be in a supermarket, but the storerooms at the back of the building would be restricted to members of staff, so any member of the public entering that 'part of a building' would become a trespasser. R v Walkington (1979) extends this example to shop counters. The defendant went behind a shop counter to look into the cash till. He was deemed to have trespassed into 'part of a building': a restricted area into which he did not have permission to go.

As a trespasser

A person entering a building without permission will be classed as a trespasser. Anyone entering with permission will not be deemed a trespasser, unless he or she goes beyond the permission that was originally given. In R v Jones and Smith (1976), one of the two defendants had permission to be in his father's house while his father was away, but neither of them had the father's permission to take his television sets and sell them. By entering with the intent of doing that, they were going beyond the permission one of them had originally been given and so they became trespassers.

Where entering a public area, such as a cinema, requires the purchase of a ticket, that ticket is regarded as a licence, giving permission to the purchaser to enter the premises and watch a film. If, however, purchasers enter the building and then go beyond this permission, for example they cause criminal damage, they will be classed as trespassers. The law is also clear where a defendant gains entry through fraud. If, for example, a defendant falsely claims to be working for a gas company but is actually entering the premises to steal, he or she has no genuine permission to be there and is therefore regarded as a trespasser.

Mens rea

There are two main parts to the *mens rea* of burglary:

- The defendant must enter as a trespasser, either knowing that he or she is trespassing or being subjectively reckless as to whether he or she is trespassing (i.e. realising that he or she may be trespassing but going ahead anyway). See R v Cunningham (1957) for a definition of subjective recklessness.
- The defendant must have the appropriate *mens rea* for the ulterior (i.e. secondary) offence with which he or she is being charged, i.e. theft, grievous bodily harm (GBH) or unlawful damage.

Note that, under s.9(1)(a) of the **Theft Act 1968**, the defendant must have the intention to commit one of the three ulterior offences at the time of entering, and here conditional intent is sufficient — it makes no difference whether or not the defendant completes the ulterior offence. Under s.9(1)(b), the defendant must also have the *mens rea* for theft or GBH when committing or attempting to commit the *actus reus* of one of these offences.

- **Enter:** entry can be effective and substantial (e.g. *R v Collins*) or effective only (e.g. *R v Brown, R v Ryan*).
- **Building or part of a building:** definition of a building is a permanent solid structure not capable of being moved (e.g. *R v Leathley* and *R v Seeking and Gould*). Part of a building is where the defendant has permission to be in one area but not another (e.g. *R v Walkington*).
- **Trespasser:** being somewhere without permission. If the defendant goes beyond the permission given this would amount to trespass

(e.g. *R v Jones and Smith*). The defendant must either intend or be reckless as to being a trespasser.

- **Mens rea:** defendant must have the *mens rea* for one of the ulterior offences as well as the intention of being reckless as to being a trespasser:
  - **9(1)(a)** intention is formed before entering a building to commit theft, criminal damage or GBH
  - **9(1)(b)** intention is formed after entering a building as a trespasser to commit or attempt to commit theft or GBH

Making off without payment

The offence of making off without payment does not appear in the **Theft Act 1968**, but was created 10 years later by s.3 of the **Theft Act 1978** to cover situations where possession of goods passes before payment is required, for example possession of petrol passing to the motorist before it can be paid for in self-service petrol stations. Section 3(1) of the **Theft Act 1978** states:

> A person who, knowing that payment on the spot for any goods supplied or service done is required or expected from him, dishonestly makes off without having paid as required or expected and with intent to avoid payment of the amount due shall be guilty of an offence.

This offence covers many different situations, such as:
- driving off without paying for petrol
- leaving a restaurant without paying for food
- running off without paying a taxi fare
- leaving a hotel without paying the bill

The offence can be broken down into *actus reus* and *mens rea*.

Actus reus

Payment required or expected

It must first be shown that a payment was required for the goods or services received. Everyone knows that if they eat in a restaurant, they should pay for the food at the end of the meal, and that if they stay in a hotel, they should settle their bill before they leave. However, if a defendant has made a prior arrangement to pay at some other time, and therefore honestly believes that payment on the spot is not required, then he or she is not guilty of making off without payment. In *R v Vincent* (2001), the defendant claimed he had made an oral arrangement with the owner of a hotel that he would pay for his stay as soon as he could after leaving. He therefore argued that payment on the spot was not required, and on appeal he was judged not guilty of

Knowledge check 15

What elements make up the *actus reus* of making off without payment?

making off without payment. The appeal court held that whether or not he made the arrangement honestly made no difference to the outcome.

Making off

If the defendant is still on the premises, he or she has not 'made off' and so cannot be guilty of this offence. In *R v McDavitt* (1981), the defendant was unhappy with the service he received in a restaurant and refused to pay the bill. When he went to leave, the manager told him the police had been called and asked him to remain in the restaurant. The defendant made his way to the toilet and remained there until the police came. He was charged with making off without payment under s.3, but the jury was told to acquit him on the basis that he had not 'made off' because he was still on the restaurant's premises. The *actus reus* of the offence had not been proved. It was, however, open to the jury to find him guilty of an *attempt* to commit the offence.

Mens rea

Knowledge that payment was required

For making off without payment to be proved, the court must be satisfied that the defendant knew that payment on the spot was required or expected for the goods supplied or services done.

Dishonesty

The test for determining whether the defendant was dishonest is the same as that used for theft under the **Theft Act 1968**.

Intent to avoid payment

Following *R v Allen* (1985), the intent must be to permanently avoid payment. If there is any intention to return and pay the amount owed, then the defendant does not have the necessary *mens rea*. In *R v Allen*, the defendant, who owed money for his stay in a hotel, left without paying, telephoning later to say he was in financial difficulties. Arrested on his return to the hotel to collect his luggage and leave his passport as security, he said he genuinely hoped to be able to pay. His conviction was quashed on appeal.

Examiner tip

When applying this offence state what the service or goods are that your defendant has received, then make sure you clearly show how your defendant made off.

Knowledge check 16

Why was the conviction in *R v Allen* quashed by the Court of Appeal?

Examiner tip

Do not confuse obtaining a service dishonestly and making off without payment. The key difference between the two is the defendant's intention before he or she obtained the goods or service. Ask yourself: did the defendant intend to avoid payment before ordering the goods (obtaining services dishonestly) or did the defendant order the goods honestly, but after realising he or she could not pay make off (making off without payment)?

Summary

- **Actus reus:** the defendant must make off — completely leave the premises (e.g. *R v Vincent*), knowing that payment is required.
- **Mens rea:** the defendant must intend to make off and must never intend to return to pay

(e.g. *R v Allen*). The *R v Ghosh* test must also be satisfied — the defendant's actions must be deemed dishonest.

Criminal damage

Three offences of criminal damage are defined in the **Criminal Damage Act 1971**:
- Section 1(1) Basic offence of criminal damage
- Section 1(2) Aggravated offence, endangering life
- Section 1(3) Criminal damage using fire (arson)

Section 1(1): basic offence of criminal damage

Section 1(1) of the **Criminal Damage Act 1971** states that a person is guilty of an offence 'who without lawful excuse destroys or damages any property belonging to another intending to destroy or damage any such property or being reckless as to whether any such property would be destroyed or damaged'.

The definition can be split up into *actus reus* and *mens rea*.
- **actus reus:** destroy or damage property belonging to another
- **mens rea:** intention to destroy or damage the property or recklessness as to whether the property would be destroyed or damaged.

Actus reus

Destroy or damage

The words 'destroy' and 'damage' are not defined in the Act, but the property will be deemed to be destroyed if it is no longer fit for its purpose, i.e. if it has been made useless. It does not have to be completely destroyed. Damage can be either permanent or temporary, and it will have occurred if time, money and effort are required to return the property to its original state. In *Roe* v *Kingerlee* (1986), mud that had been smeared on the walls of a police cell wall was held to be damage. Although the mud was not permanent, it cost money to clean it off. In *A (a juvenile)* v *R* (1978), the defendant spat on a police officer's coat, which was easily wiped off. This did not incur any expense or effort and so was deemed not to be damage.

Hardman v *Chief Constable of Avon and Somerset Constabulary* (1986) held that pavement paintings drawn with water-soluble paint constituted damage. Although the defendant claimed that the paintings would easily be washed away by rain, the local council in fact had to use water jets, thus incurring expense and effort. *Blake* v *DPP* (1993), where the defendant wrote on concrete pillars, shows that graffiti can amount to criminal damage because more often than not it can only be removed with effort and expense. It can also be important to consider what the property is used for. In *Morphitis* v *Salmon* (1990), it was held that a scratch on a scaffolding pole did not affect the usefulness of the pole.

Property

Under s.10(1) of the **Criminal Damage Act 1971**, 'property' is defined differently from how it is described in s.4 of the **Theft Act 1968**. Under the 1971 Act, it is defined as meaning:

> **Knowledge check 17**
>
> What is the definition of damage?

> **Examiner tip**
>
> When applying the *actus reus* of criminal damage make sure you say whether the item is destroyed or damaged — and remember to say why using case law.

Property of a tangible nature, whether real or personal, including money and:

(a) including wild creatures which have been tamed or are ordinarily kept in captivity, and any other wild creatures or their carcasses if, but only if, they have been reduced into possession which has not been lost or abandoned or are in the course of being reduced into possession; but

(b) not including mushrooms growing wild on any land or flowers, fruit or foliage of a plant growing wild on any land.

Belonging to another

The property that has been damaged must belong to another. No one can be guilty of criminal damage if he or she has only damaged his or her own property. Section 10(2) of the **Criminal Damage Act 1971** states that property will be treated as belonging to any person:

- having the custody or control of it
- having in it any proprietary right or interest
- having a charge on it

Mens rea

Intent or recklessness

Knowledge check 18

What must be proven to find someone reckless of causing criminal damage?

Examiner tip

Remember always to apply the *Cunningham* test — just saying the defendant is reckless is not enough for a sound answer.

For a defendant to have the necessary *mens rea*, it must be shown that he or she intended to damage or destroy the property or else was reckless as to whether the property would be damaged or destroyed. In *R v Pembliton* (1874), the defendant threw a stone at some people he had been fighting with in the street. He missed his human targets and the stone hit a window. He did not intend to damage the window and, as the jury found he was not reckless, his conviction was quashed on appeal. Recklessness is sufficient *mens rea* for criminal damage, and the test from the 1957 case of *R v Cunningham* would be applied. To be found guilty, the defendant must either know that he or she is causing criminal damage or be subjectively reckless as to whether he or she is causing it (i.e. foreseeing the risk of criminal damage occurring but going ahead anyway).

Without lawful excuse

The **Criminal Damage Act 1971** defines two lawful excuses in Sections 5(2)(a) and 5(2)(b). These act like a defence, and if the defendant is of the 'honest belief' that either of these apply, and the jury is satisfied with that honest belief, the defendant will not be held guilty.

Section 5(2)(a)

Under s.5(2)(a), if the defendant believes that the owner or guardian of the property would have consented to the damage, this is a lawful excuse for his or her actions. Section 5(3) states that it is 'immaterial' whether or not the belief is justified, so long as it is honestly held. In *R v Denton* (1982), a cotton-mill worker had set light to some of the mill machinery, damaging it and the mill building itself. His defence under s.5(2)(a) was successful because he was of the honest belief that his employer wanted him to burn down the mill, so that an insurance claim could be made on the property.

This defence can even be used if the defendant was intoxicated at the time the damage was done. In *Jaggard* v *Dickinson* (1980), the defendant caused criminal damage to what she thought was a friend's house, honestly believing that her friend would have consented to her breaking a couple of windows. Unfortunately, it turned out that the house in question belonged to someone else, and that the defendant had mistaken it for her friend's house while under the influence of alcohol. On appeal, she was judged to have 'lawful excuse' for the damage because her belief about the owner's consent was an honest one, even though formed when she was drunk.

Section 5(2)(b)

Section 5(2)(b) of the **Criminal Damage Act 1971** states that it is a lawful excuse to a charge of criminal damage if the defendant did, or threatened, the damage:

> ...in order to protect property belonging to himself or another or a right or interest in property...and at the time of the act or acts alleged to constitute the offence he believed — (i) that the property, right or interest was in immediate need of protection.

The main issue regarding this defence is that, to succeed, a defendant must believe that the property needing protection is in *immediate* danger. An example would be where a river is about to burst its banks, and the demolition of a brick wall would protect a house. The defendant would only be able to raise the lawful excuse under s.5(2)(b) if he or she had the honest belief, whether justified or not, that the house was in immediate need of protection from the floodwater.

The case of *Blake* v *DPP* (1993) raised defences under both sections 5(2)(a) and 5(2)(b). The defendant, a vicar protesting against the Gulf War, had written anti-war quotations from the Bible on large concrete pillars outside the Houses of Parliament in London. As part of his defence, he claimed that he had God's consent to the damage done, which he urged would be a lawful excuse under s.5(2)(a), and that the damage he caused was in order to protect property in the Gulf, which he hoped would be a lawful excuse under s.5(2)(b). He was convicted of criminal damage, the court holding that God could not consent to the damage, and that the damage was incapable of protecting property in the Gulf from immediate danger.

Knowledge check 19

What is the main difference between s.5(2)(a) and s.5(2)(b)?

It should be noted that 'lawful excuse' can only arise when the defendant was protecting property. It fails as a defence if the defendant was acting to protect a person. In *R* v *Baker and Wilkins* (1997), it failed because the two defendants caused criminal damage to a door when they gained access to rescue Baker's daughter.

Examiner tip

Always mention section 5 in your answers — if it is not applicable then say so.

Section 1(2): aggravated offence

Section 1(2) of the **Criminal Damage Act 1971** states:

> A person who without lawful excuse destroys or damages any property, whether belonging to himself or another:
>
> (a) intending to destroy or damage any property or being reckless as to whether any property would be destroyed or damaged; and
>
> (b) intending by the destruction or damage to endanger the life of another or being reckless as to whether the life of another would be thereby endangered;
>
> shall be guilty of an offence.

Actus reus

Destroy or damage any property

The same definitions for 'destroy' and 'damage' can be applied from s.1(1) (see page 17). 'Property' is also the same as for the basic offence, except that under s.1(2), a defendant can still be guilty if the damage or destruction is to his or her own property.

Endanger the life of another

For a defendant to be convicted, it must be his or her actual destruction of, or damage to, the property that endangers the life of another. In *R v Steer* (1987), the defendant fired shots at a house, causing damage to a door. Following an appeal to the House of Lords it was held that, for the defendant to be found guilty under s.1(2), it must be shown that the actual damage to the property endangered the life. In this case, it was held that the damage to the door did not endanger life and so the defendant was not guilty. It is worth noting that the life does not actually have to be endangered. An act capable of endangering life is sufficient for a conviction. In *R v Sangha* (1988), the defendant set fire to furniture in a neighbour's flat. The flat was empty, but the defendant was still found guilty.

Mens rea

Intent or recklessness

As with the basic offence of criminal damage under s.1(1), to be found guilty under s.1(2) the defendant must intend to destroy or damage the property or be reckless as to whether it will be destroyed or damaged. He or she must also intend the destruction or damage to endanger life, or be reckless as to whether it does. Applying the *R v Cunningham* (1957) test, to be found guilty the defendant must have realised the risk of the damage endangering the life of another. If he or she did not realise it, he or she would not be guilty.

Section 1(3): destruction or damage by fire (arson)

Section 1(3) of the **Criminal Damage Act 1971** states: 'An offence committed under this section by destroying or damaging property by fire shall be charged as arson.' The *actus reus* and *mens rea* are the same as for the basic offence in s.1(1) or for the aggravated offence in s.1(2). Note that, following *R v Miller* (1983), arson can be committed by a failure to act. The defendant accidentally started a fire, but failed to summon any help — he left the room instead. The fire spread, causing extensive damage. He was found guilty of arson under s.1(3) of the **Criminal Damage Act 1971**.

Knowledge check 20

What is the key difference between s.1(1) and s.1(2)?

Examiner tip

When applying aggravated criminal damage remember that it must be the damage to the property that could endanger the life of others — not the actions of the defendant.

Examiner tip

Always consider whether the aggravated offence can also be charged in cases of arson.

Basic criminal damage:

- *actus reus* — the defendant must destroy (make useless) or damage (taking time, money and effort to restore, e.g. *Roe* v *Kingerlee*) property, belonging to another

- *mens rea* — the defendant must intend to damage or destroy the property or be reckless as to doing so; there must be no lawful excuse for the damage: s.5(2)(a) the honest belief that the owner would consent to the damage and s.5(2)(b) the honest belief that the property was in immediate need of protection

- **Aggravated criminal damage.** The basic offence must be proven as well as proving that the damage could endanger life. The danger to life *must* come from the damage to the property (e.g. *R* v *Steer*). Lawful excuse is not applicable to aggravated criminal damage.

- **Arson.** Criminal damage with the use of fire (e.g. *R* v *Miller*) — this can be committed by a failure to act. If the offence is also aggravated s. 5 will not apply.

Fraud

Section 2: fraud by false representation

Under s.2(1), fraud by false representation is committed if a person '(a) dishonestly makes a false representation, and (b) intends, by making the representation — (i) to make a gain for himself or another, or (ii) to cause loss to another or to expose another to a risk of loss'. A representation is false if '(a) it is untrue or misleading, and (b) the person making it knows that it is, or might be, untrue or misleading'.

Actus reus

'False representation'

The word 'false' means untrue or misleading. 'Representation' means a statement, which can be express or implied, and it can relate to a matter of fact or to a matter of law. A false representation can, for example, be about identity — as when someone claims false identity in order to open a bank account. The representation can also be an omission, as where a defendant fails to declare his or her previous convictions. The representation can even be made to a machine, so it would amount to a false representation to use someone else's debit card and personal identification number (PIN) to withdraw cash from a machine without that other person's permission.

Section 2(4) states that the representation can be express or implied. An example of a representation being implied would be where a defendant used someone else's credit card, falsely representing that he or she had the authority to use it by something as simple as body language, such as a nod of the head. Note that the defendant must know that the representation is, or might be, false. He or she must know that it is someone else's credit card that is being used and that the representation being made to the shop is false.

If a defendant is using a stolen credit card, the false representation is that he or she has permission to use the card or is the named person on the card. If a defendant is using his or her own credit card, but knows that the credit limit has been exceeded,

> **Knowledge check 21**
>
> What is the difference between an express action and an implied action?

then the false representations would be that he or she had authority to use the card and that the card issuer would honour the transaction.

Mens rea

Dishonesty

As with s.2 of the **Theft Act 1968**, the two-stage test from *R* v *Ghosh* will be applied to see if the defendant acted dishonestly:

- the objective test (would a reasonable person have seen the defendant's actions as dishonest?)
- the subjective test (did the defendant realise that a reasonable person would see his or her actions as dishonest?)

If the answer to both these questions is yes, then the defendant will be held to have been dishonest. If the answer to either of the questions is no, then the defendant will be held not to have been dishonest and therefore will not be guilty of the offence.

Intending to make a gain or to cause loss

A 'gain' can be keeping something the defendant may already have, as well as getting something he or she does not have. And it can be a gain for the defendant or for another person. A 'loss' can be where someone does not get what he or she was going to get, as well as where someone parts with what he or she already had. Note that this offence is entirely offender-focused. The offence is complete as soon as a defendant makes a false representation with dishonest intent. It is immaterial whether or not anyone is aware of the representation and whether or not any property is actually gained or lost.

Section 11 Fraud Act 2006: obtaining services dishonestly

Obtaining services dishonestly is an offence under s.11(1) of the **Fraud Act 2006**, which reads: 'A person is guilty of an offence under this section if he obtains services for himself or another — (a) by a dishonest act, and (b) in breach of subsection (2).' Section 11(2) reads:

> A person obtains services in breach of this subsection if:
>
> (a) they are made available on the basis that payment has been, is being or will be made for or in respect of them
>
> (b) he obtains them without any payment having been made for or in respect of them or without payment having been made in full, and
>
> (c) when he obtains them, he knows —
>
> (i) that they are being made available on the basis described in paragraph (a), or
>
> (ii) they might be, but intends that payment will not be made, or will not be made in full

In many cases, the defendant will also have committed an offence under s.2 of the **Fraud Act 2006** (fraud by making a false representation that payment will be made

---

Knowledge check 22

What test do you apply to deem the defendant dishonest as to fraud by false representation?

Examiner tip

Always apply the *R* v *Ghosh* test in full — both the objective and subjective elements.

Examiner tip

Remember the defendant does *not* have to gain to be found guilty under s.2 of the Fraud Act 2006.

or made in full). It will be for the prosecution to decide which offence better reflects the criminality involved.

Actus reus

Obtains services for himself or another

It is not possible to commit this offence by omission. Typical examples of the *actus reus* for this offence would be pretending to be a young person or senior citizen to get reduced-price entry to an event, or using another person's membership card to get into a gym for free or at a reduced price.

Mens rea

Dishonest as to obtaining and having the intention to avoid payment in part or in full

As with s.2 of the **Theft Act 1968**, the two-stage test from *R v Ghosh* will be applied to see if the defendant acted dishonestly.

To be convicted, the defendant must intend to avoid payment in full or in part for the service provided. He or she must have that intention at the time that the service is obtained. Note that anyone ordering food in a restaurant, knowing that he or she has no money to pay for the food, is obtaining a service dishonestly. If that person then leaves the restaurant without paying, he or she will have made off without payment under s.3 of the **Theft Act 1978**.

Knowledge check 23

What is the main difference between s.11 of the Fraud Act 2006 and s.3 of the Theft Act 1978?

Knowledge check 24

What is the mens rea required to find the defendant guilty of s.11 of the Fraud Act 2006?

Examiner tip

If you think that the defendant can be charged with obtaining services dishonestly, also look for s.3 (fraud by false representation) — the two come together quite often. If the defendant has obtained the service dishonestly and then left without paying, he or she could also be charged with making off without payment.

Summary

- **Fraud by false representation:** the defendant must make a false representation (something that is untrue or misleading) — this can be implied or expressed. A false representation can be made to a machine. The defendant must be dishonest (*R v Ghosh*) as to the representation and must do it to either make a gain or cause a loss — there is no requirement that a gain or loss is in fact made.

- **Obtaining services dishonestly:** the defendant must first obtain a service. This would have been obtained in a dishonest way — the *R v Ghosh* test must be satisfied. The defendant must have the intention to avoid payment in part or full. A service *must* be obtained.

Blackmail

Blackmail is an offence under s.21 of the **Theft Act 1968**, which states: 'A person is guilty of blackmail if, with a view to gain for himself or another or with intent to cause loss to another, he makes any unwarranted demand with menaces.'

Actus reus

A demand with a menace

The defendant must make a 'demand'. This is not defined in the Act, except that it must be a demand that the victim should do — or stop doing — something. This demand can be implied or expressed, but it must be with menaces. Menaces are also not defined in the Act, and what are, or are not, menaces is an objective test, left to the jury to decide on the basis of whether a reasonable person would have been affected by the threats in the particular case. In *R* v *Clear*, it was held that the test of what constituted 'menaces' was that the threat had to be: 'of such a nature that the mind of an ordinary person of normal stability and courage might be influenced or made apprehensive so as to accede unwillingly to the demand.'

Mens rea

Defendant must intend to make a gain or cause a loss — and the demand must be unwarranted

Section 21(1) of the Theft Act 1968 states:

> A demand with menaces is unwarranted unless the person making it does so in the belief —
>
> (a) that he has reasonable grounds for making the demand; and
>
> (b) that the use of the menaces is a proper means of reinforcing the demand.

Whether the defendant believes he or she has reasonable grounds for making the demand is a subjective test, but of course the more far-fetched the belief, the less likely the jury is to believe the defendant. What matters is whether the belief was genuinely held and whether the defendant believed that the use of a threat was a proper means of enforcing the demand, e.g. *R* v *Harvey* (1980). Obviously any threat of violence cannot be a 'proper' means.

The words 'gain' and 'loss' refer 'only to gain or loss in money or other property... whether temporary or permanent' (s.34(2)). In *R* v *Bevans* (1988), the meaning of 'gain in property' was widened when an arthritis sufferer was convicted of blackmail after threatening to shoot his doctor unless he gave him a pain-killing injection.

Summary

- **Actus reus.** The defendant must make a demand to his or her victim — to do something or stop doing something. The demand can be expressed or implied. The demand must come with a menace. In *R* v *Clear*, it was held that the test of what constituted 'menaces' was that the threat had to be: 'of such a nature that the mind of an ordinary person of normal stability and courage might be influenced or made apprehensive so as to accede unwillingly to the demand'.

- **Mens rea.** The defendant, by his or her demand, must intend to make a gain or cause a loss. There is no requirement that the gain or loss is actually satisfied — it is the action of making the demand with the menace. The demand must not be unwarranted — s.21(1) of the **Theft Act 1968** states:

A demand with menaces is unwarranted unless the person making it does so in the belief —

(a) that he has reasonable grounds for making the demand; and

(b) that the use of the menaces is a proper means of reinforcing the demand.

Duress

The defence of duress (duress of threats or duress of circumstances) can be raised for all offences against property.

Duress of threats

This defence can be used where the defendant claims he or she has been forced to commit the crime by a threat of serious injury or death, e.g. *R* v *Valderram-Vega* (1985). These threats must have been made to the defendant, or his or her family or other for whom the defendant is responsible.

In *R* v *Hasan* (2005), the two key tests were laid down:
- that the defendant reasonably believed that he or she (or another) had good cause to fear serious injury or death (the subjective test)
- that a reasonable person with the same characteristics as the defendant would have responded to the defendant's belief in the same way (the objective test)

The threat must be of immediate harm (e.g. *R* v *Hasan*).

This defence will fail if:
- there was any safe avenue of escape for the defendant, for example asking the police for help
- the threat was incapable of being carried out at the time when the defendant committed the offence, e.g. *R* v *Cole* (1994)
- the defendant was not told of a particular offence that he or she was to commit, such as: 'Rob a bank' or 'Steal from that woman', e.g. *R* v *Cole*
- the duress was self-induced by the defendant's membership of a violent criminal gang because in that case, fellow gang-members' violent conduct would have been foreseeable by the defendant when he or she joined the gang, e.g. *R* v *Sharp* (1987)

Duress of circumstances

This defence is available where the defendant can reasonably claim he or she has been forced to commit a crime by the circumstance that another person has been threatened with death or serious injury.

Examiner tip

Always apply the defence last. To obtain a sound answer start by explaining how the defence works, then apply it to the scenario. This way you will make sure you include all the important elements.

Knowledge check 26

What is meant by self-induced and what is its effect on the defence of duress?

- For duress of threats to succeed the defendant must be threatened — this threat must be to cause serious injury to themselves or another, e.g. *R* v *Valderram-Vega* (1985). These threats must have been made to the defendant, or his family or other for whom the defendant is responsible.
- The threat must be of serious harm, e.g. *R* v *Hasan*.

- There must be no safe avenue of escape; the threat must be capable of being carried out (e.g. *R* v *Cole*); the threat must be to commit a specific offence (e.g. *R* v *Cole*).
- If the duress is self-induced then the defence will fail (e.g. *R* v *Sharp*).

Summary

Intoxication

Students often find the defence of intoxication difficult to deal with because the way in which it operates, if at all, depends on variables in terms of types of intoxication — whether voluntary or involuntary, whether by alcohol or illegal drugs or whether by sedative or prescribed drugs — and finally on whether the particular offence charged is an offence of basic or specific intent. Intoxication is a defence as regards offences of specific intent if it is deemed to negate that specific intent, but this is not the case for basic-intent offences. Specific-intent offences against property are theft, robbery, burglary, fraud, blackmail and making off without payment. Criminal damage is a basic-intent offence.

Knowledge check 27

What is the difference between basic- and specific-intent crimes?

Voluntary intoxication by alcohol or illegal drugs

Voluntary intoxication, following the rules under the case of *Majewski* (1977) is no defence to basic-intent crimes — these are crimes that require the lesser form of *mens rea* — recklessness. However, it can be a defence to crimes of specific intent as long as the *mens rea* for the crime is completely negated. If the *mens rea* for the offence is formed before the intoxicated state, the defence will not be available. This is shown in the case of *Attorney-General for Northern Ireland* v *Gallaher* (1963). The defendant wanted to kill his wife. He went and bought a bottle of whiskey and a knife. He became so drunk that he could not form the *mens rea* for murder, then he killed his wife. He had clearly formed the intention to kill before he became intoxicated and therefore had no defence available to him.

Voluntary intoxication using sedative drugs

If a defendant has taken drugs that normally have a sedative or soporific effect, making the user relaxed or sleepy, he or she is usually treated as being involuntarily intoxicated. In *R* v *Hardie* (1985), the defendant, after taking Valium tablets prescribed for the woman with whom he shared a flat, started a fire when she asked him to leave, and he was charged and convicted under the **Criminal Damage Act 1971**. The Court of Appeal, quashing this conviction, overturned the trial judge's direction to the jury, which had made no mention of the distinction that the law draws between dangerous/illegal and prescription/sedative drugs. The court also indicated that, in this case, the jury should have been invited to consider whether the defendant's taking of six Valium tablets was objectively reckless; following *R* v *G* (2003), the test would now be one of subjective recklessness.

Examiner tip
- Explain the rules of the defence first and then apply them to the scenario.
- Make sure you clearly state whether the defendant has committed a basic- or specific-intent crime.

Involuntary intoxication

Involuntary intoxication deals with situations where a defendant claims not to have known that he or she was taking alcohol or an intoxicating drug, because his or her food or drink was laced without his or her knowledge. The legal rule here is that, if this negates the *mens rea* of the offence, it will be a full defence to any type of offence, whether one of specific or basic intent. However, in *R* v *Kingston* (1994), which involved this defence being raised to a charge of indecent assault, the Court of Appeal allowed the defendant's appeal, holding that if a surreptitiously administered drug causes a person to lose self-control and so form an intent he or she would not otherwise have formed, the law should not hold him or her liable as the operative fault is not his or hers. This novel argument was rejected by the House of Lords, which approved the trial judge's direction to the jury that an intoxicated intent was still intent, and that the fact that the intoxication was involuntary made no difference.

Knowledge check 28

For what types of crime can you raise the defence of involuntary intoxication?

Summary

- Can be voluntary where the defendant is knowingly taking drink or drugs or involuntary where the defendant is unaware or is being forced.
- Rules under *Majewski* — the defence of voluntary intoxication is only ever a defence to crimes of specific intent. This is where the *mens rea* requires intention alone. It is *never* a defence to basic-intent crimes — those crimes requiring recklessness as *mens rea*.
- The *mens rea* must be negated for the defence to succeed — if *mens rea* is formed before the intoxication then the defence will fail (e.g. *R v Gallagher*).
- Involuntary intoxication is a defence to both specific- and basic-intent crimes. If the *mens rea* is capable of being formed the defence will fail (e.g. *R v Kingston*).
- Sedative drugs — if prescribed calming drugs are voluntarily taken and have the opposite effect then the rules of *Majewski* will not apply (e.g. *R v Hardie*).

Self-defence/prevention of crime

The defence of self-defence can be raised when a defendant is either defending himself or herself, or another, or preventing a crime.

The first requirement (as stated by Janet Loveless in *Complete Criminal Law: Test, Cases, and Materials*) is that 'defensive force will only be lawful if it is necessary, and it will only be necessary if it used to resist, repel or ward off an unjust imminent threat. The act of self-defence cannot be retaliatory or revengeful'. An attack at some future point will not be sufficiently imminent — this means 'fairly immediate'.

The second requirement is that the degree of force must be reasonable. Factors that may be taken into account in determining what is reasonable force for the purpose of both common law and statutory defences are:

- the nature and degree of force used
- the gravity of the crime or evil to be prevented
- the relative strength of the parties concerned and the number of people involved

The law does not require proportionate force, but the degree of force must be capable of being seen as only so much as is necessary to repel an attack. Excessive force will usually be evidence that the attack was retaliatory and therefore not in self-defence; see *R v Martin* (2002).

To reject self-defence as a defence, the jury must be satisfied that no reasonable person, put in the defendant's position and with the time for reflection that the defendant had, would consider the violence he or she used to be justifiable; see *Farrell* v *Secretary of State for Defence* (1980). Thus objectivity is tempered with the personal situation of the actual defendant. The test is whether the defendant used

Knowledge check 29

When can the defence of self-defence be raised?

Examiner tip

Make sure you state whether the defendant was defending him- or herself, or another, or preventing a crime — explaining what actions he or she was taking and why. Remember to say whether the force was necessary in the circumstances.

reasonable force in the 'agony of the situation' and not whether the force used would be considered reasonable by the defendant, or a reasonable person, viewing the situation in cool isolation.

Where the defendant has used excessive (and therefore unreasonable) force, neither the common law nor the statutory defence of self-defence will be open to him or her, and his or her criminal liability will be determined by his or her *mens rea* and the harm he or she has inflicted.

The law has no sympathy with drunkenness, so that an honest mistake made by a drunken defendant will render the defence of self-defence inadmissible; see *R v O'Grady* (1987).

The lawful use of self-defence is limited when it comes to protecting property.

Summary

- The defence can be raised when the defendant is defending him- or herself, or another, or preventing a crime.
- 'Defensive force will only be lawful if it is necessary, and it will only be necessary if it is used to resist, repel or ward off an unjust imminent threat. The act of self-defence cannot be retaliatory or revengeful'. An attack at some future point will not be sufficiently imminent — this means 'fairly immediate'.

- The force used by the defendant must be reasonable in the circumstances.
- To reject self-defence as a defence, the jury must be satisfied that no reasonable person, put in the defendant's position and with the time for reflection that the defendant had, would consider the violence he or she used to be justifiable.
- The law has no sympathy with drunkenness, so that an honest mistake made by a drunken defendant will render the defence of self-defence inadmissible.

Section B: Law of tort

Readers should also see the Unit 2 guide for an introduction to tort and an explanation of the rules governing liability in negligence.

Product liability

Product-liability cases in tort are subject to the ordinary rules of negligence — as in *Donoghue* v *Stevenson* (1932), where Mrs Donoghue had to prove the ginger-beer manufacturer owed her a duty of care, that he had breached that duty and the breach was the cause of her gastroenteritis and nervous shock.

A key issue in product liability is proving that the defendant's lack of reasonable care caused the defect that made the product dangerous, although the claimant does not need to prove exactly what the defendant did wrong. In *Mason* v *Williams and Williams* (1955), the claimant was injured through using a chisel that was too hard for its purpose. Although the claimant could not show any particular fault in its manufacture, he could prove that nothing had happened to it since it left the defendant's factory. This was enough to establish liability.

In a contrasting case, *Evans* v *Triplex Safety Glass* (1936), the claimant alleged that the cause of a car crash was the shattering of the windscreen, in turn caused by a defect in its manufacture. However, the judge held that the claimant had not provided sufficient evidence to satisfy the court that the manufacturers were at fault. The fault could have been unsatisfactory fitting of the windscreen by the car maker, and in any event, the claimant had owned the car for a year before the accident happened and either he or his supplier could reasonably have inspected the windscreen before the accident.

Knowledge check 30

Why was there no liability in *Evans* v *Triplex Safety Glass?*

The Consumer Protection Act 1987

Under this Act, if a claimant suffers harm as a result of a product being defective, he or she may be entitled to sue the manufacturer of that product for compensation without having to prove that the producer committed any kind of legal wrong in manufacturing that product.

What is a product?

Section 1(2) of the Act states that 'product' means any goods or electricity and includes a product that is comprised in another product, whether by virtue of being a component part or raw material. In *A* v *National Blood Authority* (2001), it was even held that contaminated blood counted as a 'product' under the Act.

Who can be a producer?

Under s.1(2), the 'producer' can be:
- the manufacturer of the actual product and also the manufacturer of a component; if a product fails because of a faulty component, both the manufacturer of the final product and the component manufacturer are liable
- the importer of a product into the EU
- any person who brand-names a product or by other means holds himself or herself out to be the producer

Under s.2(3), any supplier of a product is liable unless he or she complies with a request to name, within a reasonable time, the person supplying him or her with the product.

Knowledge check 31

Who can be a producer under the Consumer Protection Act 1987?

Defining 'defect'

This is the key concept in the Act. The defendant will be liable for damage caused wholly or in part by a 'defect' in the product. Section 3 defines a defect as existing when 'the safety of the product is not such as persons generally are entitled to expect'. Section 3(2) provides that, in assessing whether a defect exists, the court should take all the circumstances into account, including:
- the manner in which and purposes for which the product has been marketed
- the packaging of the product
- the use of any mark (e.g. the Kitemark® of the British Standards Institution) in relation to the product

- the product's instructions, or any warning about doing or refraining from doing anything in relation to the product
- what might reasonably be expected to be done with the product
- the time when the product was supplied by its producer to another

It is for the claimant to prove that, taking into account the factors above, the product is defective. Given that no product can be entirely safe, the test is whether the risk to person and property posed by the product in the context of its common use exceeds what is generally acceptable.

The following cases provide helpful illustrations of how the issue of 'defect' is treated by the courts. In *A* v *National Blood Authority* (2001), the claimants were people who had been infected with the hepatitis C virus as a result of receiving a blood transfusion. At the time, no test existed to detect whether blood donated contained that virus. The claimants sued under the **Consumer Protection Act 1987**, arguing that the blood they had been given was defective. The defendants argued that, as no test was available, the most the public could legitimately have expected was that all reasonable precautions would be taken, not that the blood would be 100% clean. However, the judge ruled that the 'avoidability' of the harm suffered by a claimant in a product liability case was not to be taken into account in judging whether the product that harmed the claimant was defective or not under the Act. He held that the blood was in fact defective, ruling that 'where, as here, there is a harmful characteristic in a non-standard product, a decision that it is defective is likely to be straightforward'.

In *Abouzaid* v *Mothercare (UK) Ltd* (2001), a 12-year-old child was injured when trying to fasten a sleeping bag (manufactured by the defendant) to the back of a pushchair. The buckle on the elastic fastenings sprang back, hitting him in the eye, causing significant loss of vision. In considering the safety that the public is entitled to expect, Pill LJ found that, although this was a borderline case, the severe consequences of the injury indicated that the product was defective. It was irrelevant whether or not this defect should reasonably have come to the manufacturer's attention.

Defences

The following defences are specified under s.4(1) of the Act, confirming that liability under the Act is not strict:

- The defect is attributable to compliance with a legal requirement.
- The defendants did not at any time supply the product to another. This proviso protects the defendants if the product has been stolen and then sold on to a customer who is injured because of a defect.
- The supply by the defendants was not in the course of business nor was it supply with a view to profit.
- The state of scientific and technical knowledge at the time when the producer put the product into circulation was not such as to enable the existence of the defect to be discovered. This is known as the 'development risks' defence.

Knowledge check 32

What is the definition of a 'defect'?

Examiner tip

In questions involving product liability, although full marks can be obtained by using either negligence (duty, breach and damage) or the Consumer Protection Act 1987, it is usually easier to obtain higher marks by using the 1987 Act and explaining/applying the rules on: product, producer, defect and the 'development risks' defence.

Medical negligence

Although in questions where it is alleged that the doctor was negligent, the basic rules of negligence apply, there are specific issues that relate to medical negligence.

Duty of care

It is not necessary to consider either the neighbour test or the incremental approach from *Caparo* v *Dickman* since it is accepted that doctors automatically owe patients a duty of care.

Breach of duty

Whether the doctor's actions or omissions resulted in a breach of duty of care will usually be the major issue in such questions. The general rule is that the doctor must have committed an act or omission that fell below the standard of care expected of an ordinary reasonable doctor at his or her level of the medical profession. Following *Nettleship* v *Weston* (1971), no allowance is made in respect of an inexperienced or trainee doctor. In *Wilsher* v *Essex Area Health Authority* (1988), a junior doctor's lack of experience was not taken into account.

The leading case on breach of duty is *Bolam* v *Friern Hospital Management Committee* (1957) in which it was ruled that 'a doctor is not negligent if he has acted in accordance with a practice accepted as proper by a responsible body of medical men skilled in that particular art'. However, in *Bolitho* v *City and Hackney Health Authority* (1997) where a 2-year-old boy died following breathing difficulties, the House of Lords decided that although the *Bolam* test was still correct law, the court did not automatically have to follow this decision just because other doctors agreed with the defendant doctor's action. Instead, the court could decide that the medical expert's opinion was not reasonable and accordingly find the doctor negligent. This decision was followed in *Marriott* v *West Midlands Regional Health Authority* (1999) where the claimant was successful in proving the GP was negligent despite there being no evidence to the contrary.

Damage and causation

The usual rules of 'but for' causation and remoteness of damage apply here, but in medical negligence questions, the issue of multiple causes may arise where there may be more than one possible cause of the claimant's condition. In such cases, the 'but for' test is modified and causation can then be established if the claimant can show that the doctor's negligence had *materially increased* the risk of injury. In *Bailey* v *MoD and Portsmouth NHS Trust* (2008), the claimant was treated at an MoD hospital before being transferred to an NHS hospital where she suffered a heart attack. She claimed that the poor treatment she received at the MoD hospital had materially weakened her and that it caused or materially contributed to her heart attack. The MoD hospital was held to be liable as its negligence had materially contributed to the claimant's resulting injury.

Knowledge check 33

In which case was a junior doctor's lack of experience ignored?

Examiner tip

In problem-solving questions where the key issue is whether the doctor has breached his or her duty of care, ensure that you consider the ruling in *Bolitho* as well as the general rule from *Bolam*.

Knowledge check 34

What causation rule was confirmed in *Bailey* v *MoD and Portsmouth NHS Trust*?

Revise the basic rules on negligence — duty of care, breach of duty, damage/causation and damages.

Product liability: the Consumer Protection Act 1987:

- Section 1(2) of the Act states that 'product' means any goods or electricity and includes a product that is comprised in another product, whether by virtue of being a component part or raw material.
- Under s.1(2), the 'producer' can be: the manufacturer of the actual product and also the manufacturer of a component or any person who brand-names a product or the importer of a product into the EU.
- Section 3 defines a defect as existing when 'the safety of the product is not such as persons generally are entitled to expect'.
- Under s.4(1) of the Act there are the following defences:
  - The defect is attributable to compliance with a legal requirement.
  - The defendants did not at any time supply the product to another.

- The supply by the defendants was not in the course of business nor was it supplied with a view to profit.
- The state of scientific and technical knowledge at the time when the producer put the product into circulation was not such as to enable the existence of the defect to be discovered — the 'development risks' defence.

Medical negligence:

- **Duty of care:** doctors and nurses automatically owe patients a duty of care.
- **Breach:** consider both *Bolam* and *Bolitho* cases, where the court could decide that the medical expert's opinion was not reasonable and accordingly find the doctor negligent.
- **Causation:** consider the multiple-cause rule. In such cases, the 'but for' test is modified and causation can then be established if the claimant can show that the doctor's negligence had *materially increased* the risk of injury.

Psychiatric injury

Historically, the law did not extend to claims brought purely in respect of psychiatric injury, mainly because psychiatric injury is difficult to diagnose, leading to the suspicion that victims might fake their symptoms and bring fictitious claims. There was also the fear of 'opening the floodgates' to numerous actions. However, this area of negligence has evolved so that various categories of people may bring a claim, provided they satisfy the additional specified legal criteria.

What is psychiatric injury?

All people who claim for psychiatric injury, whatever category they fall into, must show they are suffering from a recognised psychiatric illness, capable of resulting from the incident and recognised as having long-term effects. Mere distress, fright, grief and sorrow are insufficient. In *Reilly* v *Merseyside Regional Health Authority* (1995), where elderly visitors, suffering from angina and claustrophobia, were stuck for over an hour in a hospital lift that jammed because of negligent maintenance, it was held by the Court of Appeal that their worries about one another, and even their panic, were normal human emotions in the face of a most unpleasant experience, but they were not recognisable psychiatric injuries.

Knowledge check 35

What is the definition of psychiatric injury?

Examiner tip

In any question involving psychiatric injury, you have to define psychiatric injury and ensure that the condition from which the claimant is suffering meets this definition.

In *White and Others* v *Chief Constable of South Yorkshire Police* (1999), Lord Steyn recognised the difficulty in distinguishing between two categories of claimants: those who suffer from extreme grief and those whose suffering amounts to a medically recognisable psychiatric illness. While the symptoms could be similar and equally severe, the law provides redress only to claimants in the second category.

Primary victims

A primary victim is a person who suffers psychiatric injury — or who fears for his or her own safety — as a result of being directly affected by the negligent act. The early case law on psychiatric injury established that a person could claim if he or she were within the range of potential physical injury. In *Dulieu* v *White and Sons* (1901), the claimant suffered psychiatric injury when a horse-drawn van was driven into the public house where she was working. Kennedy LJ remarked that it was not necessary for her to have suffered physical harm through impact. It was sufficient that the psychiatric injury was caused through a 'reasonable fear of immediate personal injury to oneself'.

The distinction between primary and secondary victims was considered in some depth by the House of Lords in *Page* v *Smith* (1995). The claimant was in a car accident caused by the negligent driving of the defendant. He received no physical injury but the incident sparked a recurrence of his illness known as ME, considered by some health experts to be a mental illness. The defendant was held liable. Two important distinctions between primary and secondary victims were emphasised by the House of Lords. First, their lordships stated that the primary victim does not need to show that psychiatric injury was foreseeable, merely that some kind of personal injury was foreseeable. Once this is established, it is irrelevant whether or not the primary victim suffers physical harm as well as psychiatric harm. Second, on the issue of the recurrence of a condition to which the claimant was predisposed, they said that the primary victim does not need to be a person of normal fortitude. Commenting that someone claiming physical injury does not need to satisfy that requirement, Lord Lloyd said: 'There is no difference in principle between an egg-shell skull and an egg-shell personality.' The 'egg-shell personality' rule applies to claims for psychiatric injury; therefore, defendants must take primary victims as they find them.

Secondary victims

A secondary victim suffers psychiatric injury not as a result of being directly involved in the event or fearing for his or her own safety, but rather as a result of fearing for someone else's safety. More stringent criteria apply to secondary victims than to primary victims, not least because of the potentially endless liability that could attach to the defendant.

The law of negligence has long recognised the duty owed to secondary victims. In *Hambrook* v *Stokes Brothers* (1925), the successful claimant suffered nervous shock when she witnessed a driverless lorry careering down a narrow street in the direction of her children. Bankes LJ used as illustration a hypothetical situation in which a lorry was heading towards two mothers, each holding a baby. One suffered shock through fear for her own safety and one suffered shock through fear for the baby's safety. He questioned whether the law only allowed a claim in respect of the mother fearing for her own safety and concluded that both mothers would be able to claim. However, the

Knowledge check 36

Which case established that a primary victim could include anyone within the range of potential physical injury?

Knowledge check 37

What two important rules were laid down in *Page* v *Smith*?

Examiner tip

Usually, question scenarios deal with both primary and secondary victims — therefore, you must explain accurately why one claimant would be a primary victim.

Knowledge check 38

Why are more stringent criteria applied to secondary victims than to primary victims?

Court of Appeal stipulated that the secondary victim must perceive the event with his or her own sight or hearing.

The 'control mechanisms' applicable to secondary victims were explored thoroughly by the House of Lords in *Alcock* v *Chief Constable of South Yorkshire* (1991). This case concerned numerous claims made by relatives and friends of the 95 people killed and more than 400 people injured in the Hillsborough tragedy. The Law Lords decided that:

- The secondary victim must have close ties of love and affection with the primary victim. This is presumed between spouses and between parents and children. However, the Law Lords emphasised that close ties could exist in other kinds of family relationships and also in close friendships, but these would have to be proved by the claimant.
- The psychiatric injury must be caused through the victim's own, unaided sight and hearing of an event or its immediate aftermath. It is not sufficient to read about it or learn about it through a third party. In *Alcock*, many of the claimants had watched the disaster unfold on television, but the television companies had conformed to the television authority's code of ethics and had not shown the suffering of any recognisable individual. Consequently, it was held that the pictures televised could not be equated to sight or hearing of the event or its immediate aftermath.
- The House of Lords in *Alcock* agreed unanimously that the psychiatric injury could be caused through witnessing the immediate aftermath of the accident. The extension of the law of negligence to those who suffer psychiatric injury as a result of coming upon the immediate aftermath of an accident was settled by Lord Wilberforce in *McLoughlin* v *O'Brian* (1982). The claimant was told that her family had been involved in an accident. About 2 hours after the accident had occurred, she arrived at the hospital, where she saw her husband and two of her three children injured and covered in mud and oil. Her husband told her that their other child had been killed. The other Law Lords agreed with Lord Wilberforce that the law should be extended to cover the immediate aftermath. While it remains unclear precisely what amounts to the immediate aftermath, it appears that the victims must be in their immediate post-accident state and not, for example, nicely cleaned up.
- The psychiatric injury must be induced by shock. Lord Ackner explained this in terms of 'the sudden appreciation by sight or sound of a horrifying event, which violently agitates the mind'. Psychiatric injury caused gradually over a period of time is not recoverable. The injustice of the sudden-shock requirement is illustrated by the case of *Sion* v *Hampstead Health Authority* (1994). A father suffered psychiatric injury as a result of watching his son die over a period of 14 days. His claim was unsuccessful as the illness was not induced by shock. However, in *North Glamorgan NHS Trust* v *Walters* (2002), the Court of Appeal appears to have 'widened' this test of immediacy. Here, a 10-month-old baby was taken to hospital suffering from jaundice, and the hospital negligently underestimated the seriousness of his condition. Early next morning, the baby's mother woke to find the baby having a fit. Despite doctors' assurances, the baby died from irreversible brain damage the following day, after being transferred to a London hospital. The mother suffered a 'pathological grief reaction', and the judge awarded damages on the basis of a 36-hour-long 'shocking event'.

Knowledge check 39

What are the three key control tests from *Alcock*?

Examiner tip

All three control tests must be explained — with relevant cases — and applied. If the scenario includes an 'aftermath' issue, include an effective explanation of *McLoughlin* v *O'Brian*.

- While primary victims need only prove that personal injury, whether physical or psychiatric or both, was foreseeable, secondary victims must prove that psychiatric injury itself was foreseeable.
- It is clear from the words of Lord Lloyd (cited on page 33) that, had the claimant in *Page* v *Smith* been a secondary victim, his claim would have been unsuccessful due to his predisposition to ME. Claims by secondary victims will only be successful if the secondary victim is a person of normal fortitude.

Rescuers

The law recognises that danger invites rescue. Tortfeasors (people committing torts) are therefore expected to be liable to those who try to save their victims. In *Chadwick* v *British Transport Commission* (1967), the claimant suffered anxiety neurosis as a result of helping at the scene of a serious railway crash in which 90 people were killed. He was asked, because of his small size, to crawl into the carriages to help the injured. His claim was successful. Danger and injury to passengers were foreseeable, as were danger and injury to someone who tried to rescue them.

The question as to who qualifies as a rescuer was closely examined by the House of Lords in *White* v *Chief Constable of South Yorkshire Police* (1999). The claimants were police officers who suffered post-traumatic stress disorder as a result of helping to deal with the consequences of the Hillsborough tragedy. The Court of Appeal held that three of the police officers qualified as rescuers because they gave assistance in the immediate aftermath of the disaster. The House of Lords reversed that decision, holding that, to recover compensation for psychiatric injury, rescuers must objectively have placed themselves in danger, or reasonably have perceived themselves to be doing so. None of the claimants was exposed to danger at any time, nor did they believe that they were so exposed. They were therefore not rescuers.

Knowledge check 40

What key test for rescuers was laid down in *White* v *Chief Constable of South Yorkshire Police*?

Bystanders

The law of negligence does not allow bystanders to be compensated for psychiatric injury. As Lord Wilberforce explained in *McLoughlin* v *O'Brian* (see page 34), the law denies claims by the ordinary bystander because 'such persons must be assumed to be possessed of fortitude sufficient to enable them to endure the calamities of modern life', and because 'defendants cannot be expected to compensate the world at large'. While judges have left open the possibility of bystanders bringing claims, the courts have nevertheless been reluctant to extend the law in this way. In *McFarlane* v *E. E. Caledonia Ltd* (1994), the claimant was on a support vessel some 90 metres from the oilrig on which he normally worked when the oilrig caught fire. He helped to receive casualties by moving blankets, and assisted two of the walking wounded as they arrived on the support vessel. The claimant relied on the *obiter dicta* of Lord Keith in *Alcock*, arguing that it was difficult to imagine a more horrific disaster than the holocaust on the oilrig. The Court of Appeal held that he could not recover damages. Stuart Smith LJ said: 'The court should not extend the duty to those who are mere bystanders or witnesses of horrific events unless there is a sufficient degree of proximity, which requires both nearness in time and place and a close relationship of love and affection between claimant and victim.'

Examiner tip

If the question scenario includes a 'bystander', ensure that you explain the case of *McFarlane* to show why damages would not be paid.

- **Psychiatric injury:** a recognised psychiatric illness which occurred as a result of an accident and has long-term effects, e.g. *Reilly v Merseyside Regional Health Authority, White and Others v Chief Constable of South Yorkshire Police.*
- **Primary victims:** a person who suffers psychiatric injury — or who fears for his or her own safety — as a result of being directly affected by the negligent act, e.g. *Dulieu v White and Sons, Page v Smith.*
- **Secondary victims:** one who suffers psychiatric injury not as a result of being directly involved in the event or fearing for his or her own safety, but rather as a result of fearing for someone else's safety.
- **Control tests:** *Alcock v Chief Constable of South Yorkshire:*

- The secondary victim must have close ties of love and affection with the primary victim.
- The psychiatric injury must be caused through the victims' own, unaided sight and hearing of an event or its immediate aftermath.
- The psychiatric injury must be induced by shock.
- **Rescuers:** rescuers must objectively have placed themselves in danger, or reasonably have perceived themselves to be doing so, e.g. *Chadwick v British Transport Commission, White v Chief Constable of South Yorkshire Police.*
- **Bystanders:** the law of negligence does not allow bystanders to be compensated for psychiatric injury, e.g. *McLoughlin v O'Brian, McFarlane v E. E. Caledonia Ltd.*

Economic loss

The law of tort does not generally allow recovery of compensation for pure economic loss. However, the rules concerning when a duty of care is owed have been adapted by the courts. In limited circumstances, therefore, a claim for economic loss, suffered as a result of the defendant's negligence, may be made when the loss:

- is the direct result of damage to property or personal injury (consequential economic loss)
- is caused by a negligent misstatement
- arises from circumstances the courts have held to fall within the extended *Hedley Byrne* principle (see page 39)

As with questions that raise issues of psychiatric injury, remember that economic loss is a special duty situation within the law of negligence. A claimant will, therefore, have to prove not only that the defendant owed a duty of care, but also that there was a breach of duty, which caused the claimant's loss.

Consequential economic loss

The position, as clarified by Lord Denning MR in *Spartan Steel and Alloys Ltd v Martin and Co. Ltd* (1973), is that economic loss that is consequent upon physical damage or injury is recoverable in negligence, but there is no liability in respect of pure economic loss arising from negligent acts. In the *Spartan Steel* case, the defendants negligently severed an electricity cable supplying power to the claimants' factory. As a result, the factory had to shut down. The claimants claimed compensation for:

- damage to goods in production at the time of the power cut, i.e. physical damage
- loss of profit on the damaged goods, i.e. consequential economic loss
- loss of profit on goods that could not be manufactured due to the power cut, i.e. pure economic loss

The Court of Appeal held that compensation could be recovered for the damage to goods in production at the time of the power cut and the loss of profit that would have been made on them (which was clearly a consequence of the physical damage to the goods). However, no damage had been caused in respect of the goods that would have been manufactured later that same day. The loss of profit in respect of those goods was therefore purely economic and not recoverable.

Murphy v *Brentwood District Council* (1990) clarified the position regarding buildings and defective foundations. The claimant bought a property constructed on a concrete raft on an in-filled site. The raft foundation, which had been approved by the council, was defective and caused serious cracks to appear in the house. Unable to afford the cost (estimated at £45,000) of repairing the property to make it safe and inhabitable, the claimant sold the house at a loss of £35,000. The defendant council was held not liable for the loss. The court held that foundations of a building could not be treated as separate from the building. The building was therefore defective and the cost of repairing the building was purely economic.

Negligent misstatement

Traditionally, a claimant who suffered economic loss caused by statements would have had to bring an action in the tort of deceit. The law as it stands today developed from the dissenting judgement of Denning LJ in *Candler* v *Crane, Christmas and Co.* (1951), where the defendants, who negligently prepared a company's accounts, were aware that the accounts were to be shown to the claimant to induce him to invest in the company. The claimant lost money he subsequently invested. The court held the defendants were not liable. Denning LJ, dissenting, said the defendants owed a duty of care to their:

> ...employer or client, and...any third person to whom they themselves show the accounts, or to whom they know their employer is going to show the accounts so as to induce them to invest money or take some other action on them.

Denning LJ's dissenting judgement was accepted by the House of Lords in *obiter dicta* in *Hedley Byrne and Co. Ltd* v *Heller and Partners* (1964). A company called Easipower asked an advertising company to run a campaign. The advertising company approached Easipower's bank for a credit reference. The bank gave a satisfactory reference (including a disclaimer, i.e. a denial of responsibility) without checking the company's current financial standing. Easipower went into liquidation and the advertising company lost more than £17,000. The House of Lords held that liability for economic loss arising from a negligent misstatement could arise in such circumstances, but that in this particular case the defendants were not liable because of the disclaimer.

Special relationship

The House of Lords held that, in addition to the requirements of foreseeability, proximity and its being fair, just and reasonable to impose a duty, there must be a special relationship between the parties for a duty of care to give careful advice to arise. However, the Law Lords all gave differing accounts of what amounts to a special relationship. Lord Reid said it arises:

...where it is plain that the party seeking information or advice was trusting the other to exercise such a degree of care as the circumstances required, where it was reasonable for him to do that, and where the other gave the information or advice when he knew or ought to have known that the inquirer was relying on him. I say 'ought to have known' because in questions of negligence we now apply the objective standard of what the reasonable man would have done.

It would appear that a special relationship has three requirements:
- The defendant must possess a special skill.
- The claimant must rely on the statement to his or her detriment.
- The reliance must be reasonable.

The defendant must possess a special skill

The defendant must possess special skill in giving the advice sought. In *Mutual Life and Citizens' Assurance Co.* v *Evatt* (1971), the Privy Council held that an insurance company did not owe a duty of care in giving investment advice. A duty arose only when the defendant was in the business of giving that type of advice, or had professed to have special skill or knowledge in the field in which the advice was given. The defendant will *not*, therefore, be liable for statements made informally or in a social situation. A case which seemingly provides an exception to this is *Chaudhry* v *Prabhaker* (1988), in which the claimant had asked a friend to find a suitable car for her. The friend recommended a car, which was later discovered to have been in an accident. The decision to hold the defendant liable was justified on the basis that he should have been as careful about giving advice as he would have been if he had been buying the car for himself.

The claimant must rely on the statement to his or her detriment

In *JEB Fasteners Ltd* v *Marks, Bloom and Co.* (1983), a negligent statement was made about the value of a company's stock. The claimant did not succeed, as he had not relied on this advice. He had bought the company to secure the services of the directors, and thus placed no reliance on the value of the stock. In *Yianni* v *Edwin Evans and Sons* (1981), the claimants were purchasers of a property bought with the aid of a mortgage from a building society. The defendants were instructed by the building society to value the property so as to establish that it was worth the value of the mortgage. The defendants' valuation stated that the property was suitable as security for a loan of £12,000. The claimants relied on this favourable report, purchased the property and then discovered that it needed £18,000 worth of repairs. The High Court held the defendants liable. Park J said: 'I am sure that the defendants knew that their valuation would be passed on to the claimants and that the defendants knew that the claimants would rely on it when they decided to accept the building society's offer.' He also referred to evidence that 90% of applicants for building society mortgages over the previous 6 years had relied on building society surveys. This decision was approved by the House of Lords in *Smith* v *Eric S. Bush* (1989).

The reliance must be reasonable

The courts seem to regard such reliance as reasonable where it is foreseeable. In *Caparo Industries plc* v *Dickman* (1990), guidelines were given by the House of Lords as to when reliance may be foreseeable or reasonable. The defendant auditors were held not liable to the claimants for the negligent preparation of another company's accounts. The claimants relied on these accounts to purchase further shares in the other company and eventually take over the company. The accounts were inaccurate and misleading, and the claimants consequently incurred financial loss. Referring to the relevant case law, Lord Bridge said:

> The salient feature of all these cases is that the defendant giving advice or information was fully aware of the nature of the transaction which the claimant had in contemplation, knew that the advice or information would be communicated to him directly or indirectly and knew that it was very likely that the claimant would rely on that advice or information in deciding whether or not to engage in the transaction in contemplation.

In *James McNaughton Paper Group Ltd* v *Hicks Anderson and Co.* (1991), the facts were similar to those in *Caparo Industries plc* v *Dickman*. The defendants were accountants who prepared accounts at short notice for the chairman of a company. The accounts were then shown to the claimants who relied on them to their detriment in bidding for and taking over the company.

In that case, it was decided there was no duty owed to the claimants because the draft accounts were not prepared for their benefit and, even more importantly, the defendants would reasonably expect a party to a takeover to take independent advice and not rely solely on draft accounts.

The extended *Hedley Byrne* principle

In addition to the courts permitting recovery in negligence claims for economic loss arising from personal injury, damage to property or a negligent misstatement, there are some circumstances where liability has been imposed that does not fall squarely within these exceptions to the general rule against recovery. There does not appear to be a consistent principle applied in these circumstances, although recently there has been an attempt to fit them into the so-called 'extended *Hedley Byrne* principle'.

The difficulty has usually arisen in cases where the courts have clearly been in favour of imposing liability but there has been an absence of reliance on the part of the claimant. This was the problem facing the courts in the so-called 'wills cases'. In *Ross* v *Caunters* (1979), a solicitor prepared a will but failed to prevent its being witnessed by the spouse of a beneficiary, which rendered that beneficiary's legacy void. The would-be beneficiary successfully sued the solicitor for the economic loss sustained, although she herself had not acted in reliance on the solicitor. Sir Robert Megarry VC described the basis of the solicitor's liability to others as 'either an extension of the *Hedley Byrne* principle or, more probably, a direct application of the principle in *Donoghue* v *Stevenson*'. He explained that, where a solicitor is instructed to carry out a transaction that benefits a third party, that third party is clearly within contemplation as being likely to be affected and the fact that the loss is purely financial should be no bar to a claim.

Sixteen years later, the House of Lords approved this decision in *White* v *Jones* (1995). A testator had cut his daughters out of his estate following a quarrel. He was later reconciled with them and instructed his solicitor to prepare a new will including a

Examiner tip
The special relationship tests will be the major issues to explain and apply in problem-solving questions but some explanation/application of breach issues should also be provided, referring to the duty of a professional.

Knowledge check 43
What was the basis of the decision in *Ross* v *Caunters*?

£9,000 legacy to each daughter. The solicitor failed to act on the instructions before the testator died. The daughters' claim that the solicitor owed them a duty of care in these circumstances succeeded. Lord Goff gave the leading judgement. The problem in not allowing the claim would have been that the testator and his estate had a valid claim but suffered no loss, while the disappointed beneficiary would have suffered loss but have no claim. This would result in no potential claim against a negligent solicitor. This issue was described as 'being a point of cardinal importance in the present case'. Lord Goff said that, under the *Hedley Byrne* principle, the assumption of responsibility by the solicitor to the client should in law be held to extend to the intended beneficiary, to prevent the beneficiary from being deprived of the legacy in circumstances where neither the testator nor the testator's estate has a remedy against the solicitor.

In *Spring* v *Guardian Assurance* (1994), the issue again arose as to whether there was reliance by the claimant. The question for the House of Lords was whether an employer owes a duty of care to an employee when providing a reference for a prospective future employer. *Hedley Byrne* established that a duty of care was owed to the recipient of the reference, but the claimant was the subject of the reference and could not be said to have acted in reliance on its content. In this case, the defendant employer suggested in the reference that the employee was not honest and had little integrity, and Lord Goff had little difficulty in finding for the claimant on the basis of *Hedley Byrne*. He pointed out that an employer has special knowledge of an employee due to experience of his or her performance. Furthermore, such references are provided not only for the assistance of the prospective employer, but also to help the employee secure employment, and the employee thus relies on the employer to take care in the preparation of the reference.

Summary

Economic loss that is consequent upon physical damage or injury is recoverable in negligence, but there is no liability in respect of pure economic loss arising from negligent acts, e.g. *Spartan Steel and Alloys Ltd* v *Martin and Co. Ltd*.

- **Negligent misstatement:** special relationship requirements:
  - the defendant must possess a special skill in giving the advice sought, e.g. *Mutual Life and Citizens' Assurance Co.* v *Evatt*

- the claimant must rely on the statement to his or her detriment, e.g. *JEB Fasteners Ltd* v *Marks, Bloom and Co.*
- the reliance must be reasonable, e.g. *Caparo Industries plc* v *Dickman, James McNaughton Paper Group Ltd* v *Hicks Anderson and Co.*
- **The extended *Hedley Byrne* principle:** 'either an extension of the *Hedley Byrne* principle or, more probably, a direct application of the principle in *Donoghue* v *Stevenson*', e.g. *Ross* v *Caunters, White* v *Jones, Spring* v *Guardian Assurance*

Occupiers' liability

Occupiers' Liability Act 1957: duty owed to lawful visitors

Who is the occupier?

Section 1(2) of the 1957 Act states that the persons who are to be treated as occupiers are the same as those who would at common law have been treated as the occupiers.

The common law position is illustrated by *Wheat* v *Lacon* (1966), where the owners of a pub put it in the hands of a manager, who was authorised to take lodgers. One lodger was injured while using an unlit staircase. The House of Lords held that the owners could still be sued as occupiers because they retained some control over the state of the premises. Thus, two or more people can be occupiers. This question of 'control' is the crucial one and in each case it is a question of fact to be decided by the judge.

To whom is the duty owed?

The **Occupiers' Liability Act 1957** abolished the common law distinction between various categories of entrant and created instead a single category of 'lawful visitors', such as those who are present on the premises by the occupier's invitation, or with the occupier's express or implied permission, or in exercise of a legal right. This would include people who have received an invitation, those who have paid for the right of entry and those who visit as a result of implied permission, for example meter readers, delivery men or the fire brigade summoned to deal with a fire. Lawful authority also covers police and others exercising rights granted by warrant. Casual visitors, such as political canvassers and door-to-door salesmen, are also included.

Knowledge check 44

What is the definition of a lawful visitor?

Where is the duty owed?

The 1957 Act imposes a duty on occupiers of premises. 'Premises' is given a broad meaning by s.1(3), and may be 'any fixed or movable structure, including any vessel, vehicle or aircraft'.

What is the duty owed?

Section 2(1) provides that the duty owed is the common law duty of care. In s.2(2) this is described as:

> ...a duty to take such care as in all the circumstances of the case is reasonable to see that the visitor will be reasonably safe in using the premises for the purposes for which he is invited or permitted by the occupier to be there.

Examiner tip
This is a crucial element that must be defined accurately and then applied to the facts of the scenario.

The duty is not absolute but requires the occupier to take reasonable care. The occupier will be judged by the negligence standard: the standard of a reasonable person. The occupier's liability depends on whether he or she has done or not done what a reasonable person would have done or not done.

In *Cole* v *Davies-Gilbert* (2007), the claimant had been injured when she fell into a hole on the village green, which had been dug 2 years earlier to hold a maypole for a village fete. The hole had since been filled in and a wooden plug had been inserted, but this had been removed. The Court of Appeal rejected her claim against both the landowner and the fete organisers, holding that the standard of care under the 1957 Act was no higher than that required in common law negligence, and that both defendants had taken reasonable care.

In *Martin* v *Middlesbrough Corporation* (1965), a schoolchild slipped in the playground and cut herself on a broken milk bottle. The local council was held liable because it had not made adequate arrangements for disposing of the bottle.

In *Perry* v *Harris* (2008), where a child suffered permanent brain injury when another child on a bouncy castle hit him with his foot, the Court of Appeal decided that the parent supervising that activity was not in breach of her duty when she was distracted by another child. She had behaved as a 'reasonable person' supervising a children's party.

The duty is, however, limited in that it is only owed in respect of the purpose for which the visitor is permitted to be on the premises. No duty is owed under the Act to entrants who use the premises for other purposes. As Lord Scrutton LJ memorably said in *The Calgarth* (1927): 'When you invite a person into your house to use the stairs, you do not invite him to slide down the banisters.'

The duty owed to children

Section 2(3)(a) of the **Occupiers' Liability Act 1957** provides that an occupier must be prepared for children to be less careful than adults. The reasoning for this is that what may pose no threat to an adult may nevertheless be dangerous to a child. In *Moloney* v *Lambeth LBC* (1966), a 4-year-old fell through a gap in railings guarding a stairwell and was injured. Adults could not have fallen through the gap, so such an injury would have been impossible for them. The occupier was held liable.

Similarly, a child is unlikely to appreciate risks as an adult would, and may be attracted to the danger. Consequently, an occupier should guard against any kind of allurement that places a child visitor at risk of harm. In *Glasgow Corporation* v *Taylor* (1922), a 7-year-old ate poisonous berries in a botanical garden and died. The shrub on which the berries grew was not fenced off in any way. The corporation was held liable as it knew that the berries were poisonous and should have expected that a young child might be attracted to the shrub. The same approach was taken in *Jolley* v *Sutton LBC* (2000), where the House of Lords held the defendant liable to a 14-year-old boy who was seriously injured when an old boat fell on him. The boat was something that would be attractive to children, including those of the claimant's age, and some injury was foreseeable if children played on or around it.

The courts sometimes take the view that very young children should be under their parents' supervision. In such circumstances, the occupier will not be liable. In *Phipps* v *Rochester Corporation* (1955), a 5-year-old was injured, having fallen down a trench dug by the defendant on a piece of waste ground where the child frequently played. The defendant was not liable because the court held that the parents should have had the child under proper control.

The duty owed to experts

Section 2(3)(b) of the Act provides that an occupier may expect that a person in the exercise of his or her calling will appreciate and guard against any special risks ordinarily incident to it.

Where tradesmen fail to guard against risks that they should know about, the occupier will not be liable. In *Roles* v *Nathan* (1963), the occupier was not liable when chimney sweeps died after inhaling carbon monoxide fumes while cleaning flues. The sweeps did not accept the advice of the occupiers to complete the work with the boilers off, and in any case, should have been aware of the risks themselves. The occupier may not, however, expect experts to guard against risks not incident to their trade. Lord Denning MR pointed out that the outcome would have been different if the sweeps had been killed by a basement staircase giving way, as such a risk is not incident to cleaning chimneys.

Furthermore, the occupier may not expect experts to exercise more than the usual safeguards particular to their trade to guard against risks that are created by the occupier's own negligence. In *Ogwo* v *Taylor* (1987), a householder who started a fire by his careless use of a blowlamp was liable for injuries suffered by a fireman in fighting the blaze. Here, it was held that there was a duty owed to a rescuer by an occupier who had endangered himself or his own property as to make a rescue likely.

Knowledge check 46

Why was the householder held liable in negligence in *Ogwo* v *Taylor*?

For what damage may the occupier be held liable?

Section 1(3)(b) states that the Act applies not only to personal injury and death but also to damage to property, including property that does not belong to the visitor.

Warnings

Section 2(4)(a) provides that the occupier's liability is discharged if the occupier gives effective warning of the danger. The warning must be sufficient to enable the visitor to be reasonably safe. In *Roles* v *Nathan*, Lord Denning MR explained this section:

> Supposing for instance, that there was only one way of getting into and out of premises and it was by a footbridge over a stream which was rotten and dangerous. An occupier puts up a notice 'This bridge is dangerous'. In such a case, s.2(4)(a) makes it clear that the occupier would nowadays be liable. But if there were two footbridges, one of which was rotten, and the other safe a hundred yards away, the occupier could still escape liability, even today, by putting up a notice 'Do not use this footbridge. It is dangerous. There is a safe one further upstream'. Such a warning is sufficient because it does enable the visitor to be reasonably safe.

In some circumstances, a mere warning may be insufficient to safeguard the visitor and the occupier may be obliged to set up barriers. In *Rae* v *Mars* (1990), a warning about a deep pit inside the entrance of a dark shed was held to be ineffective. The occupier was liable. There is, however, no specific obligation to display a warning notice when the danger is one that should be obvious to any visitor. In *Cotton* v *Derbyshire Dales District Council* (1994), a walker was injured after falling from a high path along dangerous cliffs in a much-visited area. There was no notice warning of the danger. The Court of Appeal said the absence of a notice was not a breach of the common duty of care. The danger was obvious to visitors exercising reasonable care for their own safety.

Knowledge check 47

What rule does s.2(4)(a) lay down?

Negligence of independent contractors

Under s.2(4)(b), the occupier will not be liable for loss or injuries suffered by visitors when the cause of damage is the negligence of an independent contractor hired by the occupier. The reasoning behind this subsection is that the contractor will be covered by his or her own insurance.

Two requirements must be met for this section to apply:

- It must have been reasonable for the occupier to have entrusted the work to the independent contractor. In *Haseldine* v *Daw* (1941), the occupier was not liable for the negligent repair of a lift, as this was a job requiring specialist skills.
- The occupier must have taken reasonable steps to satisfy himself or herself that the contractor was competent and that the work was properly done. Only reasonable steps must be taken. If the work is of a highly complex and technical nature, it is less reasonable to impose this obligation. However, if the risk is obvious, then the occupier will be expected to discover it. In *Woodward* v *Mayor of Hastings* (1945), the occupiers were held liable when a child was injured on school steps that were negligently left icy after the contractors had cleaned off snow. The risk should have been obvious to the occupiers. Similarly, in *Bottomley* v *Todmorden Cricket Club* (2003), the claimant was injured while helping with a fireworks display on the cricket club's land, organised by an independent contractor. The club argued that since the display was organised by independent contractors, it was not liable. Dismissing the cricket club's appeal, Brooke LJ said an occupier in such circumstances can usually escape liability by showing that he or she has taken reasonable care to select competent and safe contractors. In that case, however, there was no written safety plan and the cricket club had not insisted that the independent contractor take out adequate public-liability insurance.

Knowledge check 48

Why was the cricket club held liable in *Bottomley* v *Todmorden Cricket Club*?

Defences

The occupier may raise the general defences of contributory negligence and *volenti non fit injuria* (see pages 65–66).

Occupiers' Liability Act 1984: duty owed to trespassers

The 1984 Act was passed to clarify the law relating to categories of claimant not covered by the 1957 Act. The harshness of the judicial approach in *Addie* v *Dumbreck* (1929), whereby the occupier's duty was to refrain from causing deliberate or reckless injury, was to some extent mitigated by the decision of the House of Lords in *British Railways Board* v *Herrington* (1972). A young child was injured when he gained access to an electrified railway line through vandalised fencing. Lord Diplock said the duty owed to a trespasser was limited to taking reasonable steps, such as would be taken by a person of ordinary humane feeling, to enable the trespasser to avoid the danger: the trespasser was owed the duty of 'common humanity'. Following the *Herrington* decision, the question of liability to trespassers was referred to the Law Commission, and its report in 1976 subsequently formed the basis of the **Occupiers' Liability Act 1984**.

Who is the occupier?

Section 1(2) of the 1984 Act states that the word 'occupier' bears the same meaning as under the **Occupiers' Liability Act 1957**.

To whom is the duty owed?

Section 1(1) of the 1984 Act states that the duty is owed to persons other than visitors. Usually, entrants covered by the 1984 Act will be trespassers. However, the Act also applies to people who, without the permission of the occupier, are involuntarily on the premises, to persons exercising a private right of way, and to members of the public entering under an access order or agreement made under the **National Parks and Access to the Countryside Act 1949**.

Where is the duty owed?

The duty is owed by the occupier of premises, and the meaning of premises is the same as under the 1957 Act.

In what circumstances is the duty owed?

The effect of sections 1(1) and 1(3) is that a duty is owed by a person as occupier of premises to persons other than visitors in respect of any risk of their suffering injury on the premises by reason of any danger due to the state of the premises or to things done or omitted to be done. In *Donoghue v Folkestone Properties Ltd* (2003), Lord Phillips MR said that the obvious situation in which a duty is likely to arise is where the occupier knows that a trespasser may come across a danger that is latent (concealed). In such a case, a trespasser may be exposed to the risk of injury without knowing it. But where a feature of the premises is not inherently dangerous, the 1984 Act does not impose upon an occupier a duty to prevent a trespasser from making use of that feature for an activity if it is the activity itself that causes the danger. His Lordship stressed:

> The threshold question is not whether there is a risk of suffering injury by reason of the state of the premises. It is whether there is a risk of injury by reason of any danger due to the state of the premises. Thus in order for the threshold question to be answered in the affirmative it must be shown that the premises were inherently dangerous.

In *Keown v Coventry Healthcare NHS Trust* (2006), it was ruled that the risks to the claimant had not arisen from 'any danger due to the state of the premises' but from the claimant's own misjudged actions. In that case, the claimant had climbed up a hospital fire escape, but it was held that there was nothing inherently dangerous about the fire escape.

Section 1(3) of the **Occupiers' Liability Act 1984** states that an occupier of premises owes a duty to a non-visitor if:

(a) he is aware of the danger or has reasonable grounds to believe that it exists;

(b) he knows or has reasonable grounds to believe that the other is in the vicinity of the danger concerned or that he may come into the vicinity of the danger...; and

(c) the risk is one against which, in all the circumstances of the case, he may reasonably be expected to offer the other some protection.

Knowledge check 49

What is the effect of sections 1(1) and 1(3)?

Examiner tip

In any question involving trespassers, this section is crucial. All these three rules have to be explained and applied fully.

Knowledge check 50

Which of the three rules listed on p. 45 was applied in *Swain* v *Natui Ram Pun* in dismissing the claim?

Both (a) and (b) are subjective; that is, they relate to the knowledge of the defendant. If the defendant is unaware of the danger or unaware that the person may come onto the premises, then he or she will not be liable, even if such facts would be obvious to the reasonable person. In *Swain* v *Natui Ram Pun* (1996), a child trespassing on the roof of the defendant's factory fell off and was seriously injured. Dismissing his claim, the court said the factory was surrounded by substantial fences and there was no evidence of previous trespass. Therefore, the defendant had no reasonable grounds to believe there was anyone in the vicinity of the danger. In *obiter dicta*, Pill LJ said that s.1(3)(b) imposes a subjective test based on the occupier's actual knowledge of facts giving such grounds, not on what he or she ought to have known.

The third requirement (c) is both subjective and objective. The focus is on 'all the circumstances of the case', which may include the purpose of the entry, the age and capabilities of the non-visitor and the financial resources of the occupier.

What is the duty owed?

Section 1(4) states that the duty owed by an occupier to a non-visitor is 'to take such care as is reasonable in all the circumstances of the case to see that he does not suffer injury on the premises by reason of the danger concerned'. This is a significantly lower duty than that imposed under s.2(2) of the **Occupiers' Liability Act 1957**.

In respect of what damage is the duty owed?

Section 1(1) states that the duty owed under the 1984 Act applies in respect of injury. Section 1(9) defines injury as meaning anything resulting in death or personal injury, including disease and any impairment of physical or mental condition. By virtue of s.1(8), the 1984 Act does not apply in respect of loss of, or damage to, property.

Warnings

Section 1(5) states that the occupier may discharge his or her duty 'by taking such steps as are reasonable in all the circumstances of the case to give warning of the danger concerned or to discourage persons from incurring the risk'. The level of warning required to discharge the occupier's duty under the 1984 Act is thus lower than that required under the 1957 Act. The emphasis is on making the potential entrant aware of why he or she should not come onto the premises.

Examiner tip

If a warning sign is part of the 'trespasser' scenario in an exam question, remember that the effect of a warning under s.1(5) is very different to that in the Occupiers Liability Act 1957 with respect to lawful visitors.

Defences

The occupier may raise the general defences of contributory negligence and *volenti non fit injuria* (see pages 65–66).

Occupiers Liability Act 1957, duty owed to lawful visitors:

- Occupier/control test, e.g. *Wheat* v *Lacon*.
- Lawful visitors — those with occupier's invitation, or express or implied permission, or in exercise of a legal right.
- In s.2(2) duty owed is defined as: 'a duty to take such care as in all the circumstances of the case is reasonable to see that the visitor will be reasonably safe in using the premises for the purposes for which he is invited or permitted by the occupier to be there'.
- Section 2(3)(a) provides that an occupier must be prepared for children to be less careful than adults.
- Section 2(3)(b) of the Act provides that an occupier may expect that a person in the exercise of his or her work will appreciate and guard against risks inherent in that work.
- Section 2(4)(a) provides that the occupier's liability is discharged if the occupier gives effective warning of the danger.
- Section 2(4)(b), the occupier will not be liable for loss or injuries suffered by visitors if caused by the negligence of an independent contractor hired by the occupier.

Occupiers' Liability Act 1984, duty owed to trespassers:

- Sections 1(1) and 1(3) state that a duty is owed by a person as occupier of premises to persons other than visitors in respect of any risk of their suffering injury on the premises by reason of any danger due to the state of the premises.
- Section 1(3) states that an occupier of premises owes a duty if:
  (a) he is aware of the danger or has reasonable grounds to believe that it exists;
  (b) he knows or has reasonable grounds to believe that the other is in the vicinity of the danger concerned or that he may come into the vicinity of the danger...; and
  (c) the risk is one against which, in all the circumstances of the case, he may reasonably be expected to offer the other some protection.
- Section 1(4) states that the duty owed is 'to take such care as is reasonable in all the circumstances of the case to see that he does not suffer injury on the premises by reason of the danger concerned'.
- Section 1(5) states that the occupier may discharge this duty 'by taking such steps as are reasonable in all the circumstances of the case to give warning of the danger concerned or to discourage persons from incurring the risk'.

Nuisance

Nuisance comes under three headings: private nuisance, public nuisance and statutory nuisance. This guide covers public nuisance and private nuisance in accordance with the AQA specification.

Private nuisance

In *Winfield and Jolowicz on Tort*, Professor Winfield defines private nuisance as 'unlawful interference with a person's use or enjoyment of land, or some right over, or in connection with it'.

Unlawful interference

Not all interference with enjoyment of land will constitute a nuisance. Such interference will only be unlawful if it is unreasonable. The law of nuisance thus allows for give and take.

Reasonableness in nuisance is different from the reasonableness element of negligence. In negligence, the reasonableness of the defendant's conduct is the central issue. In nuisance, the central issue is the reasonableness of the outcome of the defendant's conduct. The focus of a nuisance action is thus on the reasonableness of the interference caused to the claimant. The defendant cannot argue as a defence that he or she took reasonable care, but the conduct of the defendant is relevant in circumstances where he or she has acted maliciously.

In deciding whether the interference is unreasonable, the courts will take into account various factors:

The nature of the locality

In an industrial area, fumes are less likely to be considered unlawful interference than in a rural area. Pollock J stated in *Bamford* v *Turnley* (1862): 'That may be a nuisance in Grosvenor Square which would be none in Smithfield market.' In a residential area, cocks crowing in the morning will be more likely to be considered unlawful interference than in a rural area. In *Leeman* v *Montague* (1936), the claimant lived in a largely residential area and was regularly disturbed by the crowing of 750 cockerels on the defendant's land about 90 metres away. The court held that this constituted a nuisance.

Knowledge check 51

Which case confirmed that if physical damage is caused, the issue of location becomes irrelevant?

However, if there is physical damage to the claimant's property, then the locality issue will not absolve the defendant from liability. In *St Helens Smelting Co.* v *Tipping* (1865), the claimant bought an estate near the defendant's smelting works and suffered damage to his trees and other crops caused by the fumes. The defendants argued that there were many other smelting works in the area and so the nature of the locality prevented the interference from being unlawful. Lord Westbury LC said surrounding circumstances were relevant where enjoyment was concerned, but not where there was material damage.

Examiner tip

In many questions, this is quite a crucial issue. Therefore *consider carefully* the precise nature of the locality — residential, rural, commercial or industrial.

The duration of the harm

Generally, the more long-lasting an interference is, the more likely it will be held to be unreasonable — most nuisances will usually involve an ongoing interference, unless an isolated event actually causes physical damage. However, the duration need not last too long — in *Crown River Cruises* v *Kimbolton Fireworks Ltd* (1996), it was held that a 20-minute firework display could amount to a nuisance.

The sensitivity of the claimant

A claimant cannot put his or her land to an unusually delicate use, then complain when that land is adversely affected to a greater extent than would usually be the case by his or her neighbour's activities. In *Amphitheatres Inc.* v *Portland Meadows* (1948), the claimant's action failed when his drive-in cinema was affected by the defendant's floodlit premises. Similarly, in *Robinson* v *Kilvert* (1889), the claimant's unusually sensitive brown paper was damaged when the defendant heated his cellar, thus raising the temperature of the building. The defendant was not liable, as normal brown paper would not have been affected.

However, it should be noted that, as soon as a claimant has established that a defendant has infringed his or her right to ordinary enjoyment of his or her property, then the defendant is liable for damage due to unusual sensitivity. In *McKinnon Industries* v *Walker* (1951), the claimant's orchids were damaged and his enjoyment of his land was adversely affected by fumes and sulphur dioxide gas from the defendant's factory. The defendant argued that he should not be held liable for the damage to the orchids since growing these was a delicate operation, but the court rejected that argument, holding that, as the right to ordinary enjoyment had been infringed, the claimant could also claim for this sensitive activity.

Knowledge check 52

Why was the claimant unsuccessful in *Robinson* v *Kilvert*?

Interference with recreational amenity

In *Bridlington Relay Ltd* v *Yorkshire Electricity Board* (1965), it was held that because interference with television viewing was not a substantial nuisance, the claimants (whose business provided radio and television service to subscribers) could not sue for the business interference complained of. In *Hunter* v *Canary Wharf Ltd* (1997), it was suggested that in certain circumstances, an action for this kind of interference might be successful but that 'more is required than the mere presence of a neighbouring building.' In *Network Rail Ltd* v *Morris* (2004), the Court of Appeal accepted that Railtrack's signalling system did affect the music of the claimant's electric guitars in his recording studio, but dismissed the claim because such damage was not reasonably foreseeable.

The motive or malice of the defendant

Where the defendant's activity is motivated by malice, the courts are more likely to hold such activity to be unlawful. In *Christie* v *Davey* (1893), the claimant gave music lessons for approximately 17 hours per week. This annoyed her neighbour, who lived in the adjoining semi-detached house. He retaliated by banging trays on the wall, shouting and blowing whistles. The claimant was successful, as the defendant had acted deliberately and maliciously.

Examiner tip

If there is any evidence of malice, ensure that this is identified and explained with reference to *Christie* v *Davey*.

When the activity is motivated by malice, the defendant cannot argue that the claimant is unusually sensitive. In *Hollywood Silver Fox Farm* v *Emmett* (1936), the defendant discharged his gun on his own property in order to frighten the claimant's pregnant silverfox vixen, causing her to miscarry. Despite the delicate use of land by the claimant, the defendant's malicious intention rendered his actions a nuisance.

Courts will, however, consider the main purpose of the defendant's activity. In *Harrison* v *Southwark and Vauxhall Water Co.* (1891), it was held that the useful nature of the defendant's construction work was one reason why the claimant's action was dismissed.

Who can sue?

Anyone with a proprietary interest in the land

This will usually be the occupier, but may be a landlord who is out of possession. Members of the occupier's family cannot sue (but may sue in negligence if there is personal injury or damage to property).

An early example of this principle is provided by *Malone* v *Laskey* (1907). Mrs Malone and her husband occupied property provided by the husband's employers and sublet from Laskey who operated an engine in adjoining premises. Vibrations created by the engine caused a bracket supporting a water tank in the Malones' house to collapse and injure Mrs Malone. Although the working of the engine was a nuisance, Mrs Malone's action failed, as she had no proprietary interest in the property. This rule was upheld by the House of Lords in *Hunter* v *Canary Wharf* (1997).

The damage suffered must be of a foreseeable type

The claimant may recover damages for any foreseeable loss that he or she has suffered as a result of the nuisance. The House of Lords in *Cambridge Water Co. Ltd* v *Eastern Counties Leather plc* (1994) held that the loss suffered must be of a type that was reasonably foreseeable.

No liability in private nuisance for personal injury

Damages for personal injury are not recoverable in private nuisance. In *Hunter* v *Canary Wharf*, the House of Lords reasserted the principle that nuisance is a tort against land and not a tort against the person.

Who can be sued?

Anyone who causes a nuisance is liable for its creation and continuance. If the nuisance emanates from land, the occupier is primarily liable, and the owner not in occupation is liable only if he or she was the person who created or authorised the nuisance. An occupier is responsible for nuisances created by his or her employees, agent, family, guests and independent contractor.

Remedies

A person disturbed by a private nuisance has four main remedies open:
- damages
- an injunction
- abatement
- a complaint to the local council

Damages and injunctions

In a nuisance action, damages are often an inadequate remedy and are not usually awarded alone where the nuisance is likely to continue. In *Tetley* v *Chitty* (1986), a local council gave permission for the operation of a go-kart track on council-owned land. Three neighbours sought an injunction. McNeill J held the noise to be an inevitable consequence of the use for which permission had been given, so that the council was liable in private nuisance. Damages would have been wholly insufficient as a remedy, and an injunction was granted to restrain the council from permitting this activity. Damages may be awarded where the damage done by the nuisance is quantifiable. Damages for past loss or inconvenience may also be awarded, together with an injunction to restrain any further nuisance.

An injunction is usually the preferred remedy for the claimant, since it requires the defendant to bring the nuisance to an end. It also has the advantage of flexibility, in that it can be tailored to meet the exact circumstances of the case and produce a just solution (often a compromise). In *Leeman* v *Montague* (1936), the claimant bought a house in a largely residential area, and was regularly disturbed from 2 a.m. onwards by the crowing of 750 cockerels in the defendant's orchard about 90 metres away. The court held this activity to be a nuisance and granted an injunction restraining the defendant from carrying on his business in this manner. There was evidence suggesting that the defendant could easily rearrange his use of his land so that the birds were kept further away from the houses. Similarly, in *Kennaway* v *Thompson* (1980), the owners of a number of lakeside homes complained of the noise caused by powerboat racing on the lake. Lawton LJ granted an injunction against the race organisers, limiting both the number of days on which racing could take place and the number and power of the boats allowed to take part.

It must be remembered that the injunction is an equitable remedy and, as such, available at the discretion of the court. Where the claimant seeks an injunction, the court may decide to award damages instead if an injunction would not be in the public interest, as in *Miller* v *Jackson* (1977), where the claimant bought a house overlooking the village cricket ground. Cricket balls were frequently hit into the garden of the claimant, who sought an injunction. The Court of Appeal held the activity constituted a nuisance but declined to grant an injunction, on the basis that it would not be in the public interest to prevent the public playing cricket; instead, it awarded damages.

Abatement

Abatement is a form of self-help. A claimant is entitled to take steps to alleviate the nuisance, for example by cutting off the roots or branches of a defendant's tree that encroach onto his or her property. A claimant is even entitled, after giving due notice (except in an emergency), to enter onto a defendant's land to abate the nuisance, so long as he or she does no more damage than is strictly necessary for his or her purpose. In *Lemmon* v *Webb* (1895), branches from the claimant's trees were overhanging the defendant's land. When the defendant cut them off, the claimant sought damages. The House of Lords held that, although a person must normally give notice before taking steps to abate a nuisance, this is not necessary in an emergency or if (as here) he or she can take the necessary steps without leaving his or her own land.

Complaints to the local authority

Under s.79 of the **Environmental Protection Act 1990**, a local authority has a duty to investigate any complaints of a statutory nuisance, which the Act defines as including anything prejudicial to health or causing a nuisance arising from the state of premises, or from any accumulation or deposit thereon, or from smoke, fumes, gas, dust, steam, smells or noise emitted from them, or from any animal kept in an unsuitable place or manner. The local authority can issue an abatement order directing the occupier to eliminate the nuisance.

Public nuisance

As Professor Rogers has written: 'The essence of a public nuisance is that it is something which affects the comfort and convenience of the public as a whole rather than of an individual complainant.'

Examiner tip

The issue of what remedy is suitable is one of the most common weaknesses in nuisance questions, especially whether and what type of injunction would be appropriate. Assuming the defendant has been found liable, consider carefully how extensive an injunction needs to be. Think about the partial injunctions issued in *Leeman* v *Montague* and in *Kennaway* v *Thompson*.

Knowledge check 53

What remedy was provided in *Kennaway* v *Thompson*?

Class of people

The nuisance must affect a class of people. Romer LJ in *Attorney General* v *PYA Quarries* (1957) stated that the nuisance would affect a class of people if it was 'so widespread in its range or indiscriminate in its effects that it would not be reasonable to expect one person to take steps to put a stop to it'. In this case, the quarrying operations of the defendants, causing vibrations and dust to affect houses in the vicinity, were held to be a public nuisance.

Public nuisance is a criminal offence

In *R* v *Johnson* (1996), the defendant was convicted of public nuisance in respect of several hundred obscene telephone calls made to more than a dozen women over a period of 6 years. Upholding his conviction, Tucker J said a single call would have been a private rather than a public nuisance, but cumulatively the calls materially affected the reasonable comfort and convenience of a class of Her Majesty's subjects. The jury, properly directed, had decided that the women were sufficient in number to constitute such a class.

Public nuisance on the highway

In *Attorney General* v *Gastonia Coaches* (1977), the defendant coach operators regularly parked eight coaches on the highway outside their offices, thereby interfering with the free passage of traffic. On the application of the Attorney General, the judge granted an injunction to restrain the defendants from causing a public nuisance by their parking.

Civil proceedings

Civil proceedings to put an end to a public nuisance may be brought in the public interest by the Attorney General, by an individual with the consent of the Attorney General, or by a local authority.

Individual actions in tort: special damage

At the suit of an individual, public nuisance becomes actionable only in circumstances where particular damage is caused to an individual over and above that suffered by the general public. The claimant in a public nuisance action has to show special damage. In *Castle* v *St Augustine's Links* (1922), the claimant was driving his taxi when a ball driven from the defendant's golf course struck his windscreen and caused the loss of one of his eyes. There was evidence that balls driven from this particular tee frequently landed on the highway. This case also illustrates that damages for personal injury are recoverable in public nuisance. This was confirmed in *Corby Group Litigation* v *Corby Borough Council* (2008), where the Court of Appeal rejected the council's claim that public nuisance could not cover personal injuries.

Knowledge check 54

What rules are illustrated in *Castle* v *St Augustine's Links?*

Defences

Statutory authority

Many activities that interfere with the enjoyment of land are done by organisations operating under an Act of Parliament. Whether the defendant will be able to rely on this defence of statutory authority will depend on the discretion given to him or her by the Act of Parliament.

In *Metropolitan Asylum District* v *Hill* (1881), the defendants were given authority to build a smallpox hospital 'according to such plan, and in such manner, as they think fit'. The hospital was built in Hampstead and was held by the House of Lords to be a nuisance by virtue of its location. The defendants had the authority to build the hospital elsewhere. Similarly, in *Tate and Lyle* v *Greater London Council* (1983), the defendants were authorised by statute to design and build new ferry terminals. The defence of statutory authority partially succeeded. It was decided that some degree of siltation of the River Thames was inevitable but, if the defendants had taken reasonable care, the damage caused to the claimant's business by the siltation would have been reduced.

These cases can be contrasted with *Hammersmith and City Railway* v *Brand* (1869). The defendants had statutory authority to run trains along tracks adjoining the claimant's property. The defendants were not liable. The damaging vibration was an inevitable consequence of running the trains and an injunction would defeat the intention of the legislature. In *Allen* v *Gulf Oil Refining Ltd* (1981), the defendant company was authorised by statute to construct and operate an oil refinery. A claim in respect of the noise, smell and vibrations made by the refinery was unsuccessful as it was an inevitable consequence.

> **Knowledge check 55**
>
> Why in both these cases was the defendants not held liable in nuisance?

Planning permission

It has been argued that planning permission given by a local authority is also a defence against a nuisance action, but in *Gillingham Borough Council* v *Medway (Chatham) Dock Co.* (1992), this general argument was rejected. Here, the dock company had been given planning permission for the operation of a commercial port. Access to it was possible only via residential roads, which caused much traffic noise, and the council sued in public nuisance. The court held that the fact that planning permission had been granted for a particular activity did not mean that that activity could not give rise to liability in nuisance. However, the existence of planning permission could mean that the character of the neighbourhood had changed (from residential to commercial), which in turn could mean that what might formerly have amounted to a nuisance could now be considered reasonable. It was held that was what had happened in this case, and therefore the dock company was not liable.

Prescription

The nuisance may be legalised by the claimant tolerating the activity for more than 20 years without complaint. However, time does not begin to run until the interference reaches a sufficient degree of severity to constitute a nuisance. In *Sturges* v *Bridgman* (1879), the defendant was a confectioner who had used two large pestles and mortars on his premises for more than 20 years. The claimant built a consulting room at the end of his garden, adjacent to the defendant's premises, and at this point the noise and vibration from the defendant's activity became unacceptable. The defendant was unable to use the defence of prescription, as the nuisance had not existed until the consulting room was built. He was therefore held liable. Note that this defence is available in private nuisance but not in public nuisance.

Volenti non fit injuria

The defence of *volenti* applies when the claimant has expressly or impliedly consented to the nuisance.

Contributory negligence

The **Law Reform (Contributory Negligence) Act 1945** provides that the claimant's damages will be reduced according to his or her responsibility for the damage he or she has suffered.

Hidden, unobservable defects in property

If the defendant can be shown to have been aware of the defect, then this defence will fail. In *Leakey* v *National Trust* (1980), the surface of a hill on the defendants' land was liable to crack, and debris had occasionally fallen onto the claimant's land. During the hot summer of 1976, the defendants were asked to attend to the danger but failed to do so. A large landslip subsequently damaged the claimant's property. The claimant's action in nuisance succeeded, as the defendants were aware of the danger.

Ineffectual defences

The activity is for the public benefit

The defendant cannot argue as a defence that his or her activity is beneficial to the public. In *Bellew* v *Cement Co. Ltd* (1948), the dust and noise from a cement factory were held to be a nuisance. An injunction was granted, despite the fact that this meant closing the only cement factory in Northern Ireland at a time when there was an urgent public need for building new homes.

The claimant came to the nuisance

The defendant cannot argue as a defence that he or she was carrying on the activity complained of before the claimant moved nearby. In *Miller* v *Jackson* (1977), a housing estate was built next to a cricket ground. The claimants bought a house on the boundary of the cricket ground. They brought a successful nuisance action and were awarded damages in respect of the damage to property and interference caused by balls flying into their garden. The defendants' argument that cricket had been played on the ground for many years before the estate was built was no defence.

The defendant took all reasonable care to avoid the nuisance

Lindley LJ commented in *Rapier* v *London Tramways Co.* (1893): 'If I am sued for nuisance, and nuisance is proved, it is no defence to say and to prove that I have taken all reasonable care to prevent it.' More recently, in *Cambridge Water Co. Ltd* v *Eastern Counties Leather plc* (1994), Lord Goff stated: 'The fact that the defendant has taken all reasonable care will not of itself exonerate him.'

Examiner tip
This issue needs to be considered in any scenario where the defendant's property was built, or his activities started, before the claimant arrived on the scene.

Private nuisance:

- 'Unlawful interference with a person's use or enjoyment of land, or some right over, or in connection with it'. Such interference will only be unlawful if it is unreasonable — the focus is on the reasonableness of the interference caused to the claimant. The defendant cannot argue that he or she took reasonable care. In deciding whether the interference is unreasonable, the courts will take into account various factors:

  - **locality**, e.g. *Bamford* v *Turnley*, *Leeman* v *Montague*, *St Helens Smelting Co.* v *Tipping*
  - **duration**, e.g. *Crown River Cruises* v *Kimbolton Fireworks Ltd*
  - **sensitivity of claimant**, e.g. *Amphitheatres Inc.* v *Portland Meadows*, *Robinson* v *Kilvert*, *McKinnon Industries* v *Walker*
  - **interference with recreational amenity**, e.g. *Bridlington Relay Ltd* v *Yorkshire Electricity Board*, *Hunter* v *Canary Wharf*
  - **malice, e.g.** *Christie* v *Davey*, *Hollywood Silver Fox Farm* v *Emmett*

- **Claimant** must have proprietary interest in land, e.g. *Malone* v *Laskey*, *Hunter* v *Canary Wharf*.
- **Defendant: anyone who causes a nuisance is liable.** If the nuisance emanates from land, the occupier is primarily liable, and the owner not in occupation is liable only if he or she was the person who created or authorised the nuisance.

- **Remedies** include: damages, an injunction, abatement, a complaint to the local council.

Public nuisance:

- 'It is something which affects the comfort and convenience of the public as a whole rather than of an individual complainant.'
- The nuisance must affect a class of people, e.g. *Attorney General* v *PYA Quarries*.
- It is a criminal offence, e.g. *R* v *Johnson*.
- Public nuisance on the highway, e.g. *Attorney General* v *Gastonia Coaches*.

Defences:

- **Statutory authority**, e.g. *Metropolitan Asylum District* v *Hill*, *Tate and Lyle* v *Greater London Council*, *Allen* v *Gulf Oil Refining Ltd.*
- **Planning permission**, e.g. *Gillingham Borough Council* v *Medway (Chatham) Dock Co.*
- **Prescription**, e.g. *Sturges* v *Bridgman*.
- No defence if:
  - the activity is for the public benefit, e.g. *Bellew* v *Cement Co. Ltd*
  - the claimant came to the nuisance, e.g. *Miller* v *Jackson*
  - the defendant took all reasonable care to avoid the nuisance, e.g. *Cambridge Water Co. Ltd* v *Eastern Counties Leather plc*

The rule in *Rylands* v *Fletcher*

The rule in *Rylands* v *Fletcher* was established when the case was heard in the Court of Exchequer Chamber in 1866. The facts were that the defendants engaged a reputable firm of engineers to construct a reservoir on their land. Unknown to the defendants or their contractors, mineshafts under the defendants' land were connected to the claimant's coal mine nearby. When the reservoir was filled, water poured down the shafts and flooded the claimant's mine. Blackburn J formulated the rule in the following terms:

> The person who, for his own purposes, brings on his land, and collects and keeps there anything likely to do mischief if it escapes, must keep it in at his peril, and if he does not do so, is *prima facie* answerable for all the damage which is the natural consequence of its escape.

The rule requires the plaintiff to establish:

- a non-natural use of the land
- an escape of the thing brought onto the land
- damage caused by the escape
- that the damage suffered is of a foreseeable type

Non-natural use

In his statement, Blackburn J made clear that the rule applies where the defendant 'has brought something on his own property which was not naturally there'. This aspect of the rule was more fully explained by Lord Cairns when the case was appealed to the House of Lords. Thus, a non-natural use may be 'that which in its natural condition was not in or upon it' or, alternatively, the use may be non-natural due to quantity or volume. In *Rylands* v *Fletcher*, the bringing of water onto the land in quantities sufficient to fill a reservoir was held to be a non-natural use.

In *Rickards* v *Lothian* (1913), the Privy Council commented that a water supply to a lavatory was a necessary feature of town life and therefore a natural use. Lord Moulton commented that a water supply is 'in the interests of the community'. These words have since been subjected to judicial scrutiny. In *British Celanese Ltd* v *A. H. Hunt (Capacitors) Ltd* (1969), the defendants stored metal strips on their land. In deciding that this constituted a natural use, Lawton J, approving the 'in the interests of the community' test, commented that the metal foil was there for use in the manufacture of goods that were needed for the general benefit of the community.

The expansion of what courts considered to be 'in the interests of the community' was halted by the House of Lords in *Cambridge Water Co. Ltd* v *Eastern Counties Leather plc*, where the defendants operated a tannery and used a chlorinated solvent to degrease the pelts. The solvent seeped through the floor, and then through soil and layers of rock, and ultimately drained into the claimant's borehole just over a mile away. Consequently the claimant's water, which was destined for domestic use, became unfit for human consumption. The case was decided on the issue of foreseeability of damage. However, Lord Goff commented that, despite the facts that the chemicals were commonly used in the tanning industry and that the small industrial community was worthy of support, the storage of substantial quantities of chemicals should be regarded as an almost classic case of non-natural use.

Escape

There must be an escape from the defendant's land of the thing brought onto the land. The leading case on the requirement of an escape is *Read* v *Lyons and Co. Ltd* (1946), in which the claimant was injured by an exploding shell on the defendant's premises, where explosive shells were made. The House of Lords held the claimant's action must fail, as there had been no escape of the exploding shell from the defendant's land. Viscount Simon explained that there must be an escape from a place that the defendant has occupation of, or control over, to a place which is outside his or her occupation or control.

Knowledge check 56

In which case was the storage of large quantities of chemicals held to be a non-natural use of land?

Damage caused by the escape

Formulating the rule in *Rylands* v *Fletcher*, Blackburn J said that the defendant would be liable 'for all the damage which is the natural consequence of its escape'. Blackburn J envisaged the rule applying to all types of damage. The case of *Rylands* v *Fletcher* itself illustrates that the rule applies to damage to land.

Economic loss would also appear to fall within the rule, so long as it is direct. In *Ryeford Homes* v *Sevenoaks District Council* (1989), Judge Newey QC was of the opinion that economic loss was recoverable under the rule in *Rylands* v *Fletcher* when it was 'a sufficiently direct result of an escape of water from sewers'. The claimant in this case failed as the defence of statutory authority was successful.

Since the second half of the twentieth century, the courts have decided that the rule does not apply to personal injury. In *Transco* v *Stockport MBC* (2003), Lord Hoffmann referred to *Cambridge Water Co. Ltd* v *Eastern Counties Leather plc*, in which the House of Lords stated that the rule in *Rylands* v *Fletcher* was a special form of nuisance and concluded that personal injury was therefore not recoverable, as the rule is a tort against land.

> **Knowledge check 57**
> Which case confirmed that personal injury damages cannot be awarded in *Rylands* v *Fletcher* liability?

Damage of a foreseeable type

In formulating the rule in *Rylands* v *Fletcher*, Blackburn J stated that the defendant should 'answer for the natural and anticipated consequences'. These words indicate that liability is dependent upon the damage being foreseeable. This issue was clarified in *Cambridge Water Co. Ltd*. The House of Lords held the defendants were not liable on the basis that the harm caused to the claimant's water supply was unforeseeable. Lord Goff stated: 'Foreseeability of damage of the relevant type should be regarded as a prerequisite of liability.'

> **Examiner tip**
> This test of foreseeability must be considered in questions involving *Rylands* v *Fletcher* liability.

Who can sue?

In *Hunter* v *Canary Wharf* (1997), the House of Lords held that a claimant in the tort of nuisance must have a proprietary interest in the land affected. In *Cambridge Water Co. Ltd*, Lord Goff expressed the view that the rule in *Rylands* v *Fletcher* was an extension of the law of nuisance. The combination of these decisions leads to the conclusion that a proprietary interest in the land affected is now required by the claimant.

Who can be sued?

In Blackburn J's original formulation of the rule, the person who will be sued is the person who accumulates the particular thing that escapes. Subsequent case law seems to indicate that occupancy as well as ownership of the land falls within the rule. Lord Macmillan in *Read* v *Lyons* specifically stated that the rule in *Rylands* v *Fletcher* was 'a principle applicable between occupiers in respect of their land'.

Defences

Act of third parties

This defence will not be available where the defendant ought reasonably to foresee the actions of the third party and take steps to prevent them. In this respect, it is useful to compare *Hale* v *Jennings Brothers* (1938), where the escape of a 'chair-o-plane' from a fairground roundabout was caused by a passenger tampering with it, with *Rickards* v *Lothian* (1913), where the escape of water was due to a tap on the defendant's premises being turned on by an unknown third party. In the first case, the defence did not apply, whereas in the second one it did.

Act of God

This defence will apply where the escape is brought about by natural causes that no human foresight could have guarded against. The defence was successful in *Nichols* v *Marsland* (1876). The defendant had three artificial lakes on his land. Four bridges on the claimant's land were destroyed by flooding when the banks of the lakes burst during a violent thunderstorm. It is, however, only in rare circumstances that the defence will be successful. In *Greenock Corporation* v *Caledonian Railway Co.* (1917), unprecedented rainfall was held not to be an act of God.

Statutory authority

The success of this defence depends on whether the authority is obligatory or discretionary. In *Green* v *Chelsea Waterworks Co.* (1894), the claimant's premises were flooded when the defendants' water main burst. The defendants were not liable. They were obliged by statute to keep the water main charged at high pressure and it was inevitable that such damage would be caused by occasional bursts.

Default of the claimant

This defence applies where the damage is due to the act or default of the claimant. In *Ponting* v *Noakes* (1894), the claimant was unsuccessful when her horse stretched over to the defendant's land and ate poisonous leaves. Not only was there no escape, but the damage was caused by the actions of the claimant's horse.

Consent of the claimant

This defence applies where the claimant expressly or impliedly consents to the accumulation of the particular thing on the defendant's land. In *Peters* v *Prince of Wales Theatre (Birmingham) Ltd* (1943), the claimant leased his shop from the defendant. The shop was flooded when the sprinkler system in the adjoining theatre, also belonging to the defendant, burst. The claimant was held to have impliedly consented to the existence of the sprinkler system, which was present at the commencement of his lease.

- The tort requires the plaintiff to establish:
  - a non-natural use of the land, e.g. *Rickards* v *Lothian, Cambridge Water Co. Ltd* v *Eastern Counties Leather plc*
  - an escape of the thing brought onto the land, e.g. *Read* v *Lyons and Co. Ltd*
  - damage caused by the escape, e.g. *Ryeford Homes* v *Sevenoaks District Council, Cambridge Water Co. Ltd* v *Eastern Counties Leather plc*
  - that the damage suffered is of a foreseeable type, e.g. *Cambridge Water Co. Ltd* v *Eastern Counties Leather plc*
- Claimant must have a proprietary interest in the land affected, e.g. *Hunter* v *Canary Wharf.*
- Defendant is the occupier on whose land the mischief has accumulated.
- Defences:
  - act of third parties, e.g. *Hale* v *Jennings Brothers, Rickards* v *Lothian*
  - act of God where the escape is brought about by natural causes that no human foresight could have guarded against
  - statutory authority, e.g. *Green* v *Chelsea Waterworks Co.*
  - default of the claimant, e.g. *Ponting* v *Noakes*
  - consent of the claimant, e.g. *Peters* v *Prince of Wales Theatre (Birmingham) Ltd*

Vicarious liability

Vicarious liability is not an individual tort. It is a principle under which liability is imposed on a party in respect of torts (or crimes) committed by others. Vicarious liability arises most often in the employment relationship.

There are two key requirements for the imposition of vicarious liability on the employer. The tort (or crime) must be:
- committed by an employee
- committed in the course of the employee's employment

Who is an employee?

There is no single set test for the courts to apply in deciding whether the wrongdoer is an employee. This is due to the broad range of employment relationships that exist, and the shortcomings of the tests thus far developed by the courts.

The control test

The control test was the first attempt by the courts to establish a mechanism by which they could decide whether the wrongdoer was an employee. In *Collins* v *Hertfordshire County Council* (1947), Hilbery J explained that as the worker was an employee, the employer 'can not only order or require what is to be done but how it shall be done'. In this case, the defendants were not liable for the negligence of a surgeon that resulted in the death of a patient because Hilbery J concluded that they could not control how the surgeon was to perform his duties. This decision was much criticised in *Cassidy* v *Ministry of Health* (1951). A patient suffered permanent injury to his hand, allegedly through the negligence of the surgeon performing the operation. The surgeon was held to be the employee of the hospital authority because the hospital had the power of dismissal.

The control test nevertheless remains useful as a determining factor in some circumstances, for example when employees are hired out to work for others. In *Mersey Docks and Harbour Board* v *Coggins and Griffith* (1946), a harbour board hired out a crane and driver to the claimant under a contract, making the driver the servant of the claimant. When an accident occurred through the driver's negligence, the court held he was still effectively the servant of the harbour board. The harbour board was responsible for paying the driver, retained the power of dismissal and controlled the way the driver operated the crane. However, in *Viasystems* v *Thermal Transfer* (2005), which involved the negligence of a 'loaned employee' in fitting air-conditioning in a factory, it was held by May LJ that there was no reason in principle why both employers should not be vicariously liable if both had some control over his actions. In such a case, liability would be equally shared.

Knowledge check 58

What change in the law was made in *Viasystems* v *Thermal Transfer*?

The economic reality or multiple test

The present approach used by the courts is the economic reality or multiple test. Recognising that a single test of employment is not satisfactory, this was developed by McKenna J in *Ready Mixed Concrete* v *Minister of Pensions and National Insurance* (1968). A contract between the defendant firm and its driver provided for the driver to own his own lorry (bought with money loaned by an associated finance company). It was the responsibility of the driver to maintain the lorry and do whatever was needed to make it and a driver available throughout the contract period. McKenna J said factors to be considered when determining the existence of a contract of employment include:

- whether there is payment of a wage
- whether tools for the job are provided by the employer or the worker
- whether the worker has to obey orders
- the exercise of control over the way the work is done
- the acceptance of the business risk

No one factor is by itself conclusive. The economic-reality test has since been modified so that all factors in the relationship are considered and weighed according to their significance. Relevant factors, in addition to those mentioned above, include the method of payment, tax and National Insurance contributions and self-description.

A case illustrating the inconclusiveness of the parties' description of their working relationship is *Ferguson* v *John Dawson Ltd* (1976). The claimant was working as a self-employed labourer on a building site, which meant that he paid less income tax. When he was injured as a result of falling off the roof, the defendants argued that their duty to provide a guard rail was owed only to employees. The court held that, despite the self-description of the working relationship, the claimant was, in reality, an employee. The defendants controlled what work was done, and how and when the claimant did it.

The course of employment

The employer will be held vicariously liable for the torts (or crimes) of the employee only if at the time of the wrongdoing the employee was acting in the course of employment. There are no set criteria for determining what amounts to the course of employment; however, it is useful to consider the categories of circumstances that the courts have held to fall inside or outside its scope.

Authorised acts carried out in an unauthorised manner

Broadly speaking, this category of acts is concerned with circumstances where the employee is doing what he or she is employed to do but in a manner that has not been authorised by the employer. There are many different means by which an act may be unauthorised.

Acting over-zealously

In some situations, the act may be carried out in an unauthorised way because the employee has acted over-zealously to protect the employer's property. In *Vasey* v *Surrey Free Inns* (1996), the claimant was refused entry to a club by doormen, employees of the defendant. In a temper, the claimant kicked and damaged a glass window before walking away. The doormen chased the claimant across the car park and assaulted him with a cosh. The Court of Appeal held the club was vicariously liable for the assault. The doormen were doing their job, i.e. using force to protect their employer's property, albeit it in an excessive way.

Acting in an impliedly unauthorised way

An act may be conducted in an impliedly unauthorised way because the employer would have prohibited it, had he or she thought about it. In *Century Insurance* v *Northern Ireland Road Transport Board* (1942), an employee petrol tanker driver was delivering petrol to a garage. While the petrol was being transferred into the tankers, he lit a cigarette and negligently threw away the lighted match, causing an explosion and extensive damage. The House of Lords held the driver was acting in the course of his employment. Part of his job was to wait while the petrol was transferred. Although lighting the cigarette was for his own benefit, this was not enough to relieve the employers of their liability.

Acting in an expressly prohibited way

Sometimes the employee will perform an unauthorised act in a manner expressly prohibited by the employer. Provided the employee is doing acts he or she is employed to do, the employer will be held vicariously liable. In *Limpus* v *London Omnibus* (1862), the drivers of horse-drawn buses were expressly forbidden to race their buses, a practice engaged in by rival bus drivers in order to get custom. One driver did so and caused an accident. The company was held to be vicariously liable. The driver was doing what he was authorised to do, driving the bus, but was doing so in an expressly unauthorised manner. This case can be compared to *Iqbal* v *London Transport Executive* (1973). A bus conductor, trying to be helpful, drove a bus, despite having been forbidden to do so. His negligent driving caused damage. The employers were held not to be vicariously liable. The act of driving the bus was not an act the conductor was employed to do.

Rose v *Plenty* (1976) is another decision illustrating the courts' approach to expressly prohibited modes of performing employment duties. Against express orders to the contrary, a milkman took a 13-year-old boy to help him on his round. The boy was injured as a result of the milkman's negligent driving. The Court of Appeal held the dairy to be vicariously liable. The milkman was doing what he was employed to do, i.e. deliver milk, although in an expressly unauthorised way.

> **Knowledge check 59**
>
> Why was the milkman's employer held vicariously liable despite issuing express orders not to give lifts?

Activities outside normal hours of work

The course of employment includes not only activities carried out during normal hours of work but also activities that are closely connected. In *Ruddiman and Co. v Smith* (1889), an employee washed his hands a few minutes after his working day ended. He left the tap running and the resulting overflow damaged the claimant's adjoining premises. The court held that the negligent act was incidental to the employment and the employers were vicariously liable.

Activities of the employee while off the employer's premises may also be sufficiently related to his or her employment to fall within the principle. In *Weir* v *Chief Constable of Merseyside* (2003), an off-duty police officer was held to be acting in the course of employment when he assaulted the claimant and manhandled him down some stairs and into a police van following an argument about personal matters. The officer had identified himself to the claimant as a police officer and had acted as one, albeit badly, and that was sufficient.

Knowledge check 60

Why was the employer liable for the actions of an off-duty police officer?

Liability for employee's torts committed while travelling to and from work

The general position is that most journeys to and from work are outside the course of employment. However, journeys where employees are being paid for the time during which they travelling, and for which they are also receiving travel expenses, may be within the course of employment. In *Smith* v *Stages* (1989), an employee was injured while travelling home, due to another employee's negligent driving. The employees had worked 24 hours without a break and decided to drive straight back home, having had no sleep. The employees were paid wages to cover the journey time and had been given expenses to cover a return rail fare. The House of Lords held the employer to be vicariously liable.

Where the employee is outside the scope of employment

The employer will not be vicariously liable for activities performed by the employee that have no relevance to the job he or she is employed to do. In these circumstances, the employee is said to be 'on a frolic of his own'. In *Heasmans* v *Clarity Cleaning* (1987), the defendants were contracted to clean the claimant's offices. A cleaner employed by them used the claimant's telephones to make long-distance calls costing a total of about £1,400. The defendants were not vicariously liable. While the cleaner's employment had put him in the position to make the calls, it was a wholly unauthorised act and therefore not in the course of his employment.

When employees who travel from place to place as part of their job take a detour for their own benefit, they are acting outside the course of employment. In *Storey* v *Ashton* (1869), a wine merchant's driver and clerk went out to deliver some wine and collect empty bottles. On the way back, they took a detour in order to fetch a cask belonging to the clerk, and ran over the claimant. The claimant sued for damages. The court held the employer was not vicariously liable. The driver was not on his employer's business at the time of the accident, but on 'a frolic of his own'.

Close connection between the wrongful act and the employee's work

Often, employees do work which they have no express authority to do, but which is performed in order to further some objective of their employer. Unless the employee has acted so outrageously that no employer could reasonably be assumed to have accepted such an act as being within the scope of employment, the employer will be liable for torts thus committed. This liability extends to criminal conduct as illustrated in *Lister* v *Hesley Hall Ltd* (2002), where the employee was a warden living in a boarding house attached to the school run by the defendant company. The warden had sexually assaulted boys at the school without the knowledge of the defendant. The boys concerned sued the defendant for damages on the basis that the company was vicariously liable for the torts committed by the warden. The House of Lords held the defendant was vicariously liable because there was a sufficiently close connection between the work the warden had been employed to do and the acts of abuse that he had carried out. Another reason for imposing this liability was that the tort constituted a particular risk that was inextricably linked to the employer's business. Substantially the same decision was reached in the 2012 case of *JGE* v *the Trustees of the Portsmouth Roman Catholic Diocesan Trust* where a priest had sexually abused a young girl and *Maga* v *Archbishop of Birmingham* (2010).

Summary

- Vicarious liability is not an individual tort — it is a principle under which liability is imposed on a party in respect of torts (or crimes) committed by others. It arises most often in the employment relationship.
- The tort (or crime) must be:
  - committed by an employee
  - committed in the course of the employee's employment
- To determine whether the tortfeasor is an employee the following tests may be used:
  - control test, e.g. *Collins* v *Hertfordshire County Council*, *Cassidy* v *Ministry of Health*
  - the economic reality or multiple test, e.g. *Ready Mixed Concrete* v *Minister of Pensions and National Insurance*, *Ferguson* v *John Dawson Ltd*
- The employee must be acting in the course of employment.

- Authorised acts carried out in an unauthorised manner:
  - acting over-zealously, e.g. *Vasey* v *Surrey Free Inns*
  - acting in an impliedly unauthorised way, e.g. *Century Insurance* v *Northern Ireland Road Transport Board*
  - acting in an expressly prohibited way, e.g. *Limpus* v *London Omnibus*, *Iqbal* v *London Transport Executive*, *Rose* v *Plenty*
- Activities outside normal hours of work, e.g. *Ruddiman and Co.* v *Smith*, *Weir* v *Chief Constable of Merseyside*.
- Liability for employee's torts committed while travelling to and from work, e.g. *Smith* v *Stages*.
- Where the employee is outside the scope of employment, e.g. *Heasmans* v *Clarity Cleaning*, *Storey* v *Ashton*.
- Close connection between the wrongful act and the employee's work, e.g. *Lister* v *Hesley Hall Ltd*, *JGE* v *the Trustees of the Portsmouth Roman Catholic Diocesan Trust*, *Maga* v *Archbishop of Birmingham*.

General defences

Throughout this guide, the defences specific to particular torts have been considered in context. There are, however, also general defences, which are applicable to most torts. The AQA specification requires students to consider the general defences of contributory negligence and *volenti non fit injuria*.

Contributory negligence

Until 1945, contributory negligence was a complete defence. Negligent defendants could avoid paying any compensation if they could show that the victim had in some way contributed to his or her loss. The injustice caused to such victims prompted Parliament to remedy the situation by passing the **Law Reform (Contributory Negligence) Act 1945**. Section 1(1) of the 1945 Act provides:

> Where any person suffers damage as the result partly of his own fault and partly of the fault of any other person, a claim in respect of that damage shall not be defeated by reason of the fault of the person suffering the damage, but the damages recoverable in respect thereof shall be reduced to such extent as the court thinks just and equitable having regard to the claimant's share in the responsibility for the damage.

The effect of the 1945 Act is that contributory negligence is a partial defence, which, if proved, results in the claimant's damages being reduced according to his or her responsibility for the loss suffered. The wording of s.1 is focused on the damage suffered by the claimant. Lord Denning MR in *Froom* v *Butcher* (1975) said: 'The question is not what was the cause of the accident, it is rather what was the cause of the damage.' This point is clearly illustrated by some of the road-traffic accident cases in which the defence has succeeded. In *O'Connell* v *Jackson* (1972), a moped driver was injured while not wearing a crash helmet. Damages were reduced by 15%. In *Froom* v *Butcher*, the claimant was not wearing a seat belt and was injured in an accident caused by the defendant. Damages were reduced by 25%. In neither of these cases was the accident caused by the negligence of the claimant, but in each case their injuries were more serious due to the failure to take reasonable care for their own safety.

Emergencies

The requirement placed on the claimant to take reasonable care for his or her safety is important in the context of emergency situations. Any action taken by the claimant that is reasonable in the agony of the moment and that results in injury to himself or herself will not amount to contributory negligence. In *Jones* v *Boyce* (1816), the claimant jumped from a coach when he saw that it was in imminent danger of overturning due to the breaking of a coupling rein. He broke his leg. The coach was then halted safely. The court held that the claimant had acted reasonably in the agony of the moment and could therefore recover damages in full.

Children

There is no clear indication in the 1945 Act as to the age at which children can be guilty of contributory negligence. Nor can any set guidelines on specific age limits be

Examiner tip

Always consider contributory negligence in questions involving trespassers.

Knowledge check 61

What important point did Lord Denning make about contributory negligence in *Froom* v *Butcher*?

gleaned from the case law, although the decisions do give some indication of future outcomes. For example, in *Snelling* v *Whitehead* (1975), the House of Lords was clear that contributory negligence would have been irrelevant as the claimant was only 7 years old, but in *Morales* v *Eccleston* (1991), the Court of Appeal held the 11-year-old claimant to be 75% responsible for his injuries. He had run out into a road without looking and was struck by a car.

Volenti non fit injuria

The Latin maxim *volenti non fit injuria* is usually translated as 'voluntary assumption of risk'. Unlike contributory negligence, *volenti* is a complete defence and, if established, will result in the victim receiving no compensation.

The essential elements are that the victim:
- knows of the risk of injury
- voluntarily decides to take the risk
- expressly or impliedly agrees to waive any claim in respect of such injury

Knowledge of the risk

A person cannot be *volenti* to a risk of which he or she has no knowledge, even if it can be shown that a reasonable person would have been aware of the risk. In *Murray* v *Harringay Arena* (1951), a 6-year-old spectator was injured when an ice-hockey puck was struck out of the rink. Due to the likelihood of risk, the claim against the organisers failed on the basis that there was no breach of duty. However, the Court of Appeal commented that a 6-year-old could not have knowledge of the risk attributed to him. The defence of *volenti* was, therefore, irrelevant. The requirement of knowledge is also illustrated by the case of *Vine* v *Waltham Forest LBC* (2000). The claimant had become ill while driving and needed to vomit. She left her car in a private car park for a short while and returned to find it clamped. The defence did not apply because the claimant had no knowledge of the risk of the car being clamped. She had not, in her distressed condition, seen the warning notices.

Knowledge check 62

What is the general rule about knowledge of risk?

Mere knowledge of the risk does not constitute consent

It is important to note the distinction between knowledge and consent. It cannot necessarily be said that a person consents to a risk of injury merely because he or she is aware of it. This aspect of the defence was emphasised by the House of Lords in *Smith* v *Baker* (1891). The claimant and other employees were aware that a crane often swung heavy stones above them as they worked, although no warning was given to the employees of particular times at which the crane would be operating. The claimant was injured when a stone from the crane fell on him. The House of Lords held the defence of *volenti* did not apply. Lord Herschell said mere continuance in service with knowledge of the risk did not constitute consent.

Consent must be given voluntarily

For consent to be voluntary, a person must be in a position to choose freely. He or she must have full knowledge of the relevant circumstances and there must be no constraints that might interfere with freedom of will. In *Morris* v *Murray* (1990), the claimant was a passenger in a light aircraft being flown by his friend. Both men had been drinking before boarding the plane. The aircraft crashed, killing the pilot and seriously injuring the claimant. The defence of *volenti* succeeded. The claimant had knowingly and willingly gone on a flight with a drunken pilot and there had been no compulsion to do so.

It is clear that an employee's perception of the likely effect of his or her actions on employment prospects may constitute a feeling of constraint that interferes with his or her freedom of choice. One case where there was said to be no such interference was *Imperial Chemical Industries Ltd* v *Shatwell* (1965). The claimant and his brother were shot firers employed by the defendants. They decided to test a circuit of detonators, ignoring the employer's usual safety procedures and warnings, and were both injured. The dangers of not taking precautions had been highlighted to them by their employers, and employees who continued to disobey instructions had been sacked. The House of Lords allowed the defence of *volenti* to succeed. The defence is also likely to succeed where the claimant is employed to do work that necessarily involves danger. In *Bowater* v *Rowley Regis Corporation* (1944), Goddard LJ gave working in an explosives factory as an example where there would always be a risk of explosion, even when all statutory provisions were observed.

A further category of cases in which the claimant may be said to voluntarily assume the risk of injury is sporting cases. The principle applied by the courts is that the claimant, whether a spectator or a participant, consents only to the risks ordinarily incidental to the particular sport. In *Wooldridge* v *Sumner* (1963), the claimant, a photographer, was struck by a horse competing at an equestrian event. The rider had, in an error of judgement, taken a corner too fast. The defence of *volenti* applied. However, in *Condon* v *Basi* (1985), the defence did not apply. The claimant sustained a broken leg as the result of a tackle by the defendant, which was said by the referee to constitute foul play. The defendant was liable on the basis that a footballer consents only to tackles that the rules of the game permit.

Rescue cases

The courts take a more sympathetic approach to rescuers because the law should not discourage people from helping those in danger. In *Haynes* v *Harwood* (1935), a policeman was injured while attempting to stop a horse bolting along a busy street. The Court of Appeal rejected the *volenti* defence. The claimant had taken a personal risk in order to eliminate the danger to others in the street. The same approach was adopted by the Court of Appeal in *Baker* v *Hopkins* (1959), where a doctor, knowing the risk, insisted on going down a well to try to help workmen overcome by carbon monoxide fumes. The doctor was also overcome by the fumes and died. The *volenti* defence was rejected and the doctor's widow succeeded in her claim.

Remedies

The AQA specification requires students to acquire an outline knowledge of civil remedies. Questions will sometimes specifically ask for consideration of the remedies available to the claimant. This is particularly so with nuisance questions (which usually require a brief explanation and application of both injunctions and damages) and negligence and occupiers' liability questions (which usually require a brief explanation and application of damages).

Examiner tip

Consider the possibility of *volenti* as a defence in questions involving trespassers.

Knowledge check 63

Why did the defence of *volenti* succeed in *Morris* v *Murray*?

Damages

You should revisit the pages in the Unit 2 guide dealing with damages. It is important that you are able to explain and apply the concepts of general and special damages, and pecuniary and non-pecuniary losses, and that you can consider how the courts calculate damages using the multiplier and multiplicand. Reference may also be made in the exam to provisional damages and structured settlements.

Injunctions

The injunction is an equitable remedy and, as such, available at the discretion of the court (unlike damages, which are available as of right to the successful party). The court will take into account equitable principles such as 'Let right be done' and 'He who comes to equity must come with clean hands'. When answering an exam question, it is therefore important that students recognise that the behaviour of the defendant may be relevant in this area.

An injunction is a court order ordering the defendant *not* to do something. There must be a strong probability of grave damage to the claimant and damages must be an inadequate remedy. The likelihood of hardship to the defendant is also taken into account. Prohibitory injunctions are frequently imposed in cases involving trespass or nuisance, the idea being that the defendant should not be able to buy the right to commit a tort. Hardship to the defendant is not considered.

Injunctions may be sought in both public and private nuisance actions. In *Attorney General* v *PYA Quarries* (see page 52), the Attorney General successfully brought an action to restrain the activity of PYA Quarries on behalf of local residents who were disturbed by vibrations and dust. The injunction may be granted to limit the activity of the defendant rather than prevent it altogether, as shown in *Leeman* v *Montague* and *Kennaway* v *Thompson*. Although the public interest is not considered in deciding whether an activity constitutes a nuisance, the courts do consider it when determining whether the claimant should be awarded an injunction, as in *Miller* v *Jackson*.

Summary

Defences:

- **Contributory negligence: Law Reform (Contributory Negligence) Act 1945:**
  - results in the claimant's damages being reduced according to his or her responsibility for the loss suffered, e.g. *Froom* v *Butcher*, *O'Connell* v *Jackson*
  - emergencies — any action taken by the claimant that is reasonable in the agony of the moment and that results in injury to himself or herself will not amount to contributory negligence, e.g. *Jones* v *Boyce*
  - children — compare the cases of *Snelling* v *Whitehead* and *Morales* v *Eccleston*

- ***Volenti non fit injuria*:**
  - knows of the risk of injury, e.g. *Murray* v *Harringay Arena*, *Vine* v *Waltham Forest*, *Smith* v *Baker*
  - voluntarily decides to take the risk, e.g. *Morris* v *Murray*, *Imperial Chemical Industries Ltd* v *Shatwell*, *Condon* v *Basi*
  - expressly or impliedly agrees to waive any claim in respect of such injury
  - rescue cases, e.g. *Haynes* v *Harwood*, *Baker* v *Hopkins*

Remedies:
- damages
- injunctions

Questions & Answers

How to use this section

This section of the guide provides you with questions that cover the Unit 4 topics: Criminal Law (Offences Against Property) and Tort Law (each separate tort and any appropriate defences). Each question is followed by an A-grade answer, which demonstrates both the structure that you should employ and how to use case and statutory authorities.

Note particularly the importance of using cases effectively. Failure to do this is probably the most significant difference between A-grade and C-grade answers.

To acquire the necessary skills and become more familiar with this style of examination question, you should practise adapting the A-grade answers to different scenarios. You are also strongly encouraged to download past papers and mark schemes from AQA (**www.aqa.org.uk**) or to obtain these from your teacher. Studying the reports written by the chief examiner after each examination will provide considerable assistance in pinpointing the weaknesses that commonly occur in the different questions and identifying how to address these.

The mnemonic **IDEA** may help you to answer scenario-based problem-solving questions:

I   **Identify** all the relevant criminal law and tort actions and their possible defences.

D   **Define** the key legal elements of each of these.

E   **Explain** in detail the various legal rules.

A   **Apply** these rules to the facts of the scenario, using authorities (both case law and statutes) to support your answer.

Examiner's comments

Each question is followed by a brief analysis of what to watch out for when answering it (shown by the icon ⓔ). The student answers are accompanied by examiner's comments (preceded by the icon ⓔ). These help explain the elements of the answer for which marks can be awarded and are intended to give you an insight into what examiners are looking for.

Assessment objectives

Assessment objectives (AOs) are common to AS and A2 units and are intended to assess students' ability to:
- recall, select, deploy and develop knowledge and understanding of legal principles accurately, and by means of examples
- analyse legal material, issues and situations, and evaluate and apply the appropriate legal rules and principles

- present a logical and coherent argument and communicate relevant materials in a clear and effective manner, using correct legal terminology

Examination technique

Planning

Lack of planning will almost certainly result in one grade being lost or, in this paper, more probably two. Once you have decided which question to answer, make a detailed plan for both parts (a) and (b) before you start to write your answer to (a). Re-read the scenario to ensure that all key issues have been identified, and then consider which are the most important and relevant cases.

Case references

The importance of case references cannot be overemphasised in this unit. A case-free answer would be fortunate to achieve even an E-grade pass. Without appropriate case references, it is not possible to demonstrate a sound understanding of relevant law. Never forget that the cases you have been taught do not just illustrate that rule of law; in most cases, they *are* the law.

Application

As chief examiners' reports clearly indicate, a failure to apply the law to the particular facts in the scenario remains a key weakness in many students' answers. To answer these questions effectively requires much more than restating the relevant rules together with case references. The rules must be applied to the actual scenario facts so as to demonstrate a fuller understanding.

Omissions

Omission of one or more relevant legal topics is the greatest single source of lost marks. Spend time reading the question carefully and deciding which legal topics are relevant to the scenario — in many cases, there will be more than one topic.

Quality of written communication marks

Each A2 paper carries 5 marks for quality of written communication (QWC). The easiest way to lose some of these marks is to misspell basic legal words such as burglary, sentence, trespasser, vicarious, negligence and nuisance.

Section A

Question 1 Theft, robbery and fraud

> Des, who had a violent and unpredictable personality, saw Eddie in the street and called him over. Eddie, who was 16 years old and who knew Des, was frightened when Des showed him a knife and told him to 'get some money for me from a few old ladies'. Des also said that he would be watching Eddie all the time. Eddie managed to get money from a number of old people in the street, either by telling them that he was homeless and needed money for food, or, if they refused his request, by persistently asking in an increasingly aggressive manner. Des took the money with him to a bar where he drank a large amount of beer. He managed to get his last pint of beer without paying by allowing the barman to believe that he was part of a larger crowd who had ordered a lot of drinks.
>
> Adapted from AQA examination paper, January 2008

> **Discuss the possible criminal liability of Eddie for property offences arising out of his collection of money from the old people, and of Des arising out of the way in which he got his last pint of beer without paying.**
>
> (25 marks)

e As with all such scenario 'problem-solving' questions, you are required to identify relevant legal issues, to define and explain relevant legal rules and then to apply these to provide (for a sound response) 'a sustainable analysis leading to satisfactory conclusions'. You need to use cases effectively to explain rules.

A-grade answer

Eddie could be charged with theft for taking the money. Theft is defined under s.1(1) of the Theft Act 1968: 'A person is guilty of theft if they dishonestly appropriate property belonging to another with the intention of permanently depriving the other of it'.

Eddie has appropriated (by assuming the rights of an owner under s.3 of the Act) money ('property' under s.4) that belonged to the old people ('property belonging to another' as defined in s.5). Under the test established in *R v Ghosh*, he assumed these rights in a dishonest way because it can be argued that, according to the ordinary standards of reasonable and honest people, what was done was dishonest, and Eddie must have realised that what he was doing was by those standards dishonest. Nor do his actions come within the descriptions of appropriation that are not to be regarded as dishonest under s.2 of the 1968 Act. Eddie also had the intention of 'permanently depriving' the old people of their money under s.6. So clearly this is a completed theft.

e Always start by proving a completed theft — it is easier to do this then raise it to robbery.

The charge of theft could then be raised to robbery as force was used. Section 8(1) of the Theft Act 1968 states: 'A person is guilty of robbery if he steals, and immediately before or at the time of doing so, and in order to do so, he uses force on any person or puts or seeks to put any person in fear of being then and there subjected to force.'

The *actus reus* for robbery is the completed theft and the use of force or the threat of force immediately before or at the time of stealing. When some of the old people refused his initial request, Eddie became increasingly aggressive, and a jury may decide that this aggressive manner amounted to a threat of force. The relevant words of s.8(1) here are 'uses force on any person or puts or seeks to put any person in fear of being then and there subjected to force'. Whether Eddie's behaviour comes within that section is a question of fact for the jury. The other part of the statutory definition — 'he steals, and immediately before or at the time of doing so, and in order to do so, he uses force' — will have been met by Eddie's action in this case as, if there was a threat, it appears to have been immediately before the theft. The *mens rea* is that Eddie must intend to use the force to steal — when the old people refused to give him the money he became aggressive. This clearly shows that it was his desired consequence to use the force to steal. The key is that, to be found guilty, the defendant must either have put the victim in fear or have sought to put the victim in fear, and it does not matter by what means this is achieved.

(e) The answer includes good evidence to back up the explanation of the law. It is always a good idea to read your answer back — can you work out what is going on in the scenario? If you can then your evidence is sufficient, if not then you need to bring in more evidence in order to obtain full marks.

Eddie also obtained some money by claiming he was homeless and needed money for food. These claims may have been true, but it is clear from the scenario that they were not Eddie's motivation on this occasion. If they were false, Eddie could be charged under s.2 of the Fraud Act 2006 with dishonestly making a false representation, intending to make a gain for himself or another (in this case, Des). The dishonesty test here is again the *Ghosh* test. In obtaining the money in this way, Eddie could also be guilty of theft under s.1(1) of the Theft Act 1968 for dishonestly appropriating property belonging to another with the intention of permanently depriving the other of it. Section 1(2) of the Theft Act 1968 states that it is immaterial whether dishonest appropriation is made with a view to gain or is made for the thief's own benefit.

Eddie's best defence to charges of robbery, fraud or theft may be duress of threats, which can be used where a defendant claims he or she has been forced to commit the crime by a threat of serious injury or death. Being threatened with a knife, as in the present scenario, is certainly a threat of serious harm. The threat must be to commit a specific offence, and Eddie was told by Des to get some money from a few old ladies, which meets that requirement. The defence fails if there was a safe avenue of escape for Eddie, but Des said that he would be watching him, so no escape was possible. The threat must have been capable of being carried out at the time when the defendant committed the offence, and that appears to have been the case here. The jury will have to be satisfied that the defendant reasonably believed he had good cause to fear serious injury or death (the subjective test); and that a reasonable person with the same characteristics as the defendant would also have believed this (the objective test). It would certainly seem fair for a jury to find that Eddie felt threatened by Des and did fear for his safety and that a reasonable person of the same age as Eddie (16 years old) would also have felt threatened. However, Eddie may be under a disadvantage from the House of Lords decision in *R* v *Hasan* (2005), where it was held that a person voluntarily associating with known criminals ought reasonably to foresee the risk of future coercion.

(e) This is an effective explanation of the rules on duress with good application — the reference to the decision in *Hasan* is particularly relevant here.

In relation to Des's last beer, he allowed the barman to believe he was with a large group of people in the bar, although Des well knew that he was not with this group and clearly intended to make a gain. This is fraud by false representation under s.2 of the Fraud Act 2006. Section 1(4) makes it clear that a false representation under the Act may be express or implied. From the scenario, it sounds as if Des's representation was implied, but either way (express or implied) it is covered by the terms of the statute.

Leaving a bar without paying for one's drink also amounts to theft under s.1(1) of the Theft Act 1968 ('A person is guilty of theft if he dishonestly appropriates property belonging to another with the intention of permanently depriving the other of it'). Des clearly appropriated the beer (property), which belonged either to the bar or to the large group of people who may have ended up paying for it. He would probably be found to have done this in a dishonest way because, applying the *Ghosh* test, it could be argued that, according to the ordinary standards of reasonable and honest people, what was done was dishonest, and, leaving aside for a moment the issue of his drunken state (which I will return to below), Des must have realised that what he was doing was by those standards dishonest. He clearly had the intention to permanently deprive another of the beer.

Not paying for the drink could also make Des liable for the offence of making off without payment under s.3 of the Theft Act 1978. A person is guilty under that section if, knowing that payment on the spot for any goods supplied or service done is required or expected, he or she dishonestly makes off without having paid as required or expected and with intent to avoid payment. Des clearly knew the beer should have been paid for there and then, but he left the premises never intending to return and pay.

As Des had been drinking, he may be able to raise the defence of intoxication. Voluntary intoxication is where a defendant has knowingly taken drink or drugs. The case of *DPP* v *Majewski* (1976) held that this defence is only available where crimes of specific intent (i.e. where a specific intent is an essential element of the offence) are involved. The three crimes with which Des might be charged — fraud, theft and making off without payment — are all crimes of specific intent, so the defence could apply to this scenario. For it to succeed, however, a defendant's *mens rea* has to have been completely negated by the effect of the alcohol. In other words, the degree of intoxication has to be extreme. This would be an issue for the jury to determine in the present case. As it is clear that Des was not so obviously drunk that the barman refused to serve him, it could well be that the defence would fail.

(e) This is a straightforward analysis of the key elements of intoxication — voluntary intoxication by alcohol and the recognition that all relevant offences are ones of specific intent. The legal rule in such cases is both clearly stated and applied.

(e) **25/25 marks awarded. This is a good, comprehensive answer. The offences of theft, robbery and fraud by false representation are all clearly identified, explained and applied. The structure is good. The student begins by explaining the offence, clearly giving the definition. The answer then breaks it down into clear elements — first explaining the *actus reus*, followed by the application, and then explaining the *mens rea*, again followed by the application. All the offences are well applied with excellent use of evidence to enhance the answer. The defence of duress is correctly raised, and the issue of the defence possibly failing because of the self-induced element is dealt with well. The defence of intoxication in relation to Des is explained well, and the rules are made clear and are applied well. The answer leaves the question of whether the defence will succeed for the jury to decide.**

Question 2 **Burglary and criminal damage**

Des left the bar to visit a female friend. However, he had only been to her house once before and he became confused between a number of houses. Finally, though he was wrong, he was certain that he had found his friend's house. No one seemed to be in, but he managed to go through an unlocked door from the garage into the house. Inside, he began to play about, lighting paper with his cigarette lighter. Eventually, the carpet was set alight, and he hastily smothered it with a cushion. The cushion was badly damaged. When Des woke up in the house next morning, he was confronted by the owner, Fred, who was returning from work. Des ran out, barging into Fred on the way. Fred was knocked down and suffered a broken arm.

Adapted from AQA examination paper, January 2008

Discuss the possible criminal liability of Des arising out of the incidents at the house.   **(25 marks)**

(e) As with all such scenario 'problem-solving' questions, you are required to identify relevant legal issues, to define and explain relevant legal rules and then to apply these to provide (for a sound response) 'a sustainable analysis leading to satisfactory conclusions'. You need to use cases effectively to explain rules.

A-grade answer

On the facts, it seems likely that Des would be charged with causing criminal damage to both the carpet and the cushion under the Criminal Damage Act 1971 s.1(1). The *actus reus* required under the statute is 'without lawful excuse' destroying or damaging 'any property belonging to another'. Des has clearly damaged a carpet that belongs to Fred. In relation to the cushion that was badly damaged when Des smothered the carpet fire with it, Des could argue that he had a lawful excuse under s.5 of the 1971 Act. This excuse is available if defendants have destroyed or damaged property in order to protect property belonging to themselves or another, and at the time believed that the property was in immediate need of protection and the means adopted were reasonable in all the circumstances. The only issue here is whether Des's use of the cushion to smother the fire was reasonable. In the absence of a fire extinguisher or ready access to water, such an action could well be held to be reasonable by a jury.

(e) The offence is well explained and legal terms are defined clearly. Lawful excuse is explained well and the issue of whether the actions were reasonable is discussed well.

The *mens rea* of this offence is either intention to destroy or damage property (desired consequence) or subjective recklessness. In this case, it seems more likely that Des's conduct was reckless — conscious taking of an unjustified risk — but the jury would have to decide whether or not he realised the risk when he was playing about with his lighter. It could also be argued that Des committed the further offence of aggravated criminal damage under s.1(2) of the 1971 Act, since causing a house fire can endanger people's lives. It is not a requirement that life should actually be endangered — this was confirmed in *R* v *Parker*, where, as here, there was no one else in the house.

(e) This is good application of recklessness. It clearly applies the rules of *Cunningham* and does not simply say that Des was reckless.

The requirement for *mens rea* means that a defendant must have intended to endanger life (or been reckless as to endangering life) by the damage. Again, it could be argued that Des's actions in playing about with his lighter were reckless. As the property damage was done by fire, Des could also be charged with arson under s.1(3). Des had drunk 'a large amount of beer', so may try to plead intoxication in his defence. However, both s.1(1) and s.1(2) offences are held to be offences of basic intent only. Under the rule established in *R* v *Majewski*, voluntary intoxication, whether by alcohol or illegal drugs, cannot be pleaded to such offences.

In relation to Des's entry to the wrong house, he could be charged with burglary. For this charge to succeed under section 9 it must be proven that Des entered, a building, as a trespasser. He has clearly entered a building — a house is a solid structure. His entry will be deemed substantial and effective (*Collins*).

(e) Burglary is introduced well. The student clearly states the elements of the *actus reus* and applies each in turn.

Under s.9(1)(a) of the Theft Act 1968, it has to be proved he entered as a trespasser with intent to steal, commit unlawful damage or inflict grievous bodily harm. Under s.9(1)(b), having entered as a trespasser, he will have to have stolen something or inflicted or attempted to inflict grievous bodily harm on any person in the building. There are difficulties in proving either of these offences. While Des certainly entered the building as a trespasser, he will not be found guilty unless he intended to trespass or was reckless as to whether he was doing so. It is clear that an honest belief in a right of entry will negate the necessary *mens rea*. However, as he had only visited his friend's house on one previous occasion, it could be argued that he would have been unable to form an honest belief that he had a right to enter when she was not there — but that is a question to be decided by the jury.

It seems that, at the time of entry, he had no intention to commit any of the three offences specified in s.9(1)(a). However, there is a greater chance of a conviction under s.9(1)(b), so long as Des is found to have the necessary *mens rea* for trespass, because, having entered as a trespasser, he then inflicted grievous bodily harm on Fred.

Des could possibly raise the defence of intoxication. Intoxication is where the defendant is under the influence of either drink or drugs. The intoxication can be either voluntary (the defendant has knowingly taking the drink/drugs) or involuntary (defendant either does not know or has been forced). Under the rules of *Majewski* voluntary intoxication is only ever a defence to specific intent crimes — those are crimes where intention alone is required. Voluntary intoxication is never a defence to basic intent crimes — those crimes requiring recklessness.

Des is clearly voluntarily intoxicated and therefore applying the rules of *Majewski* he will only be able to raise intoxication to crimes of specific intent.

To the charge of criminal damage he will not be able to raise the defence as it is a basic intent crime. However, it may be that the rules under *Jaggard and Dickinson* could be applied regarding the lawful excuse and intoxicated mistake.

However, the charge of burglary, being a specific intent crime, could give rise to intoxication as a defence. But it must be satisfied that his *mens rea* for such an offence was completely negated. The fact he fell asleep straight after the event may indicate this, but he did try to put the fire out and this could indicate that he was aware of what he was doing.

ⓔ The defence of intoxication is well explained and applied. The offences have been identified as either basic or specific and the rules of the defence applied accordingly. There is good use of evidence to come to a coherent conclusion.

ⓔ **25/25 marks awarded. All relevant potential offences are clearly identified and explained. The explanations give definitions of legal terms and use case law to back these up. The application is clear, and the *mens rea* is applied well — the student applies the full test of recklessness with confidence. The issue of intoxication is raised and the student gives an accurate account of the legal approach, demonstrating a good understanding of the difference between basic and specific intent offences. The student raises the issue of mistake and brings in the case of *Jaggard and Dickinson*.**

Question 3 Theft, fraud, obtaining services dishonestly and making off without payment

Uma and Violet were employed by Warren. One day at work, Uma discovered that Violet had left her purse in the toilets. Uma removed a fitness club membership card from the purse and then put the purse in the wastepaper bin (from which it was later removed and returned to Violet by an alert colleague). Uma subsequently used the membership card to get herself a training session at the fitness club, for which she would normally have had to pay £10. She quietly dropped the card at the reception desk when she left.

Adapted from AQA examination paper, January 2007

Discuss Uma's criminal liability for a range of property offences arising out of the incidents involving the purse and the use of the membership card.

(25 marks)

ⓔ As with all such scenario 'problem-solving' questions, you are required to identify relevant legal issues, to define and explain relevant legal rules and then to apply these to provide (for a sound response) 'a sustainable analysis leading to satisfactory conclusions'. You need to use cases effectively to explain rules.

A-grade answer

Uma's criminal liability regarding the purse and membership card amounts to theft. Under s.1(1) of the Theft Act 1968: 'A person is guilty of theft if he dishonestly appropriates property belonging to another with the intention of permanently depriving the other of it.' In this scenario, Uma has appropriated the purse and card within the definition in s.3 of the Act because she has assumed 'the rights of an owner' over them. Both items are clearly tangible items and would be deemed as personal property under section 4, and both the card and purse did not belong to Uma. All the elements of the *actus reus* therefore seem to have been met.

ⓔ The offence of theft is clearly defined and all elements of the *actus reus* are well applied using legal terminology.

Before Uma can be found guilty, it must be shown that she had the necessary *mens rea*, i.e. was dishonest in appropriating these items as, clearly, her actions do not fall within s.2's definitions of appropriations that are not to be regarded as dishonest. Applying the *R v Ghosh* test, what she did was dishonest, according to the ordinary standards of reasonable and honest people, and she must have realised that what she was doing was by those standards dishonest.

Her borrowing of the membership card brings her within the scope of s.6(1) of the Act: 'A person appropriating property belonging to another without meaning the other permanently to lose the thing itself is nevertheless to be regarded as having the intention of permanently depriving the other of it if his intention is to treat the thing as his own to dispose of regardless of the other's rights; and a borrowing or lending of it may amount to so treating it if, but only if, the borrowing or lending is for a period and in circumstances making it equivalent to an outright taking or disposal.' As for the purse, although she did not keep it, by disposing of it she treated it as if she was the owner. She could therefore be convicted of theft under s.1(1) as regards both the purse and the membership card.

ⓔ The *mens rea* is well explained and s.2 in particular is well applied using the *R* v *Ghosh* test.

By going on to use the membership card to gain entrance to the gym and benefit from a training session normally costing £10, she led the gym to believe that she had purchased the card, which she had not. Thus criminal liability would arise under the Fraud Act 2006, s.2, as she obtained the session by an implied false representation. She had the necessary *mens rea* for this offence as she knew that the representation was untrue or misleading and she made it with intent to make a gain or cause loss — this was using the gym. To be found guilty under s.2(1)(a), she would have to have acted dishonestly — applying the *R* v *Ghosh* test, what she did was clearly dishonest by gaining access with someone else's card, according to the ordinary standards of reasonable and honest people, and she must have realised that what she was doing was by those standards dishonest — she was fully aware the card was not hers.

ⓔ The use of the card amounts to a false representation. This is defined clearly and applied well, showing that the representation was implied. The *R* v *Ghosh* test is also applied well.

As, after using the gym, Uma left without paying for a service that required payment, she could also be regarded as having obtained a service dishonestly — by using someone else's gym card, and so could be charged with that offence under s.11 of the Fraud Act 2006. The necessary *mens rea* is knowing that the service does require payment, coupled with dishonesty and the intent to avoid full or part payment at the time of obtaining the service. Uma is clearly aware that payment is expected and she was dishonest in her actions — a reasonable person would deem the use of someone else's card as dishonest and Uma realised this.

ⓔ This is clear and well laid out — the offence is clearly defined and the application is precise.

She could also be found liable for the offences of obtaining services by deception under s.1 of the Theft Act 1978 or of making off without payment under s.3 of that Act. Making off without payment is where the defendant knows that an on-the-spot payment is required for a service or goods given, but makes off, leaving the premises (as defined in *R* v *McDavitt*), intending never to pay. Following the case of *R* v *Allen* the intent must be to permanently avoid payment. Uma has clearly left the gym not paying the £10 required, she has clearly made off. From the scenario it would indicate that she had no intention to return to pay so therefore satisfies both the *actus reus* and *mens rea*.

ⓔ This section makes excellent use of the scenario when applying the law. Note that making off without payment, fraud by false representation and obtaining services dishonestly appear together — this is very common.

ⓔ **24 or 25/25 marks awarded. This is a sound answer. It is well structured, with a clear application of law to facts. The answer rightly identifies a number of different possible offences, defines each of the statutory offences well and then applies the law to the facts. It correctly explains that Uma could be charged with theft of both the purse and the membership card, even though the purse was eventually returned to Violet. The use of the membership card is clearly identified as a fraudulent offence, Uma having made a false representation. Finally, the options of Uma being charged with obtaining a service dishonestly, obtaining services by deception or making off without payment are well explained.**

Question 4 Theft, making off without payment, robbery, the defence of intoxication

Sam had been drinking heavily in a bar. When he left the bar, he wandered unsteadily into a shoe shop and tried on a pair of shoes. Before anyone realised what had happened, he had walked out of the shop and down the street, still wearing the shoes. Eventually, Trisha, a shop assistant, ran after him. However, Sam would not be persuaded that they were not his shoes. He pushed Trisha away roughly and walked on a little further before suddenly collapsing in a drunken stupor. By now, the shoes were scratched and could no longer be sold at full price.

Adapted from AQA examination paper, January 2007

Discuss Sam's possible criminal liability for property offences in connection with the incidents involving the shoes.

(25 marks)

ⓔ As with all such scenario 'problem-solving' questions, you are required to identify relevant legal issues, to define and explain relevant legal rules and then to apply these to provide (for a sound response) 'a sustainable analysis leading to satisfactory conclusions'. You need to use cases effectively to explain rules.

A-grade answer

Sam could be held liable for the theft of the shoes. Under s.1(1) of the Theft Act 1968, a person is guilty of theft if he or she dishonestly appropriates property belonging to another with the intention to permanently deprive the other of it. The shoes are the property of the shop and Sam has clearly appropriated them — treated them as his own. Applying the *R* v *Ghosh* test, it could be argued that, according to the ordinary standards of reasonable and honest people, what was done was dishonest, and, leaving aside the issue of his drunken state, Sam must have realised that what he was doing was by those standards dishonest.

🅔 The explanation of the offence of theft is concise but accurate. It is defined and all elements have been applied well.

By wearing the shoes when he left the shop, Sam was making off without payment — an offence under s.3 of the Theft Act 1978. To find a defendant guilty under s.3, it must be shown that he or she knew an on-the-spot payment for goods was required but nevertheless made off, i.e. left the premises, without paying for the item. To be found guilty, the defendant has to intend not to pay but also know that payment was meant to be made. Sam must have known that he should have paid for a pair of shoes, but he left without paying and it appears from the scenario that he did not intend to return, so he is likely to be found guilty of this offence.

We are told that a shop assistant followed him out of the shop and Sam pushed her away roughly. This could give rise to the offence of robbery. Section 8 of the Theft Act 1968 provides that a person may be guilty of robbery if immediately before or at the time of the theft he or she applied force in order to steal. There must first be a completed theft — we have already proven this above — Sam stole the shoes. We now need to prove that there was force. For a prosecution to be successful, the force must have been applied before or at the time of taking the shoes — and in order to take the shoes. Theft can, however, be regarded as a continuing act (see the case of *R* v *Hale*), so Sam's 'rough push' could be judged to have happened while the theft was still ongoing. The push certainly amounts to force, as the slightest touch is enough (see *Corcoran* v *Anderton*).

🅔 The student has identified the issue of an ongoing theft correctly and applied it using case law. It is worth noting that if any GBH appears in the scenario it would mean that one of two offences needs to be discussed — either robbery or burglary.

Sam could also face a charge of criminal damage under s.1 of the Criminal Damage Act 1971 because the shoes have been scratched. A defendant is guilty of this offence if he or she destroys or damages property belonging to another, with the intent to cause such damage, or being reckless as to whether damage is caused, and without any lawful excuse. As the shoes can no longer be sold at the same price, this will amount to damage — as it would take time, money and effort to restore them. The shoes are tangible property belonging to the shop, and although Sam may not have intended to cause this damage, he was clearly reckless in his actions and took an unjustified risk (see the contrasting cases of *R* v *Pembilton* and *R* v *Cunningham*). He must have thought about the possible risk that his actions could result in damaging the shoes, but went ahead with his actions anyway.

Sam could possibly raise the defence of intoxication. Intoxication is where the defendant is under the influence of either drink or drugs. The intoxication can be either voluntary (the defendant has knowingly taking the drink/drugs) or involuntary (defendant either does not know or has been forced). Under the rules of *Majewski*, voluntary intoxication is only ever a defence to specific-intent crimes — those are crimes where intention alone is required. Voluntary intoxication is never a defence to basic-intent crimes — those crimes requiring recklessness.

The defence of intoxication is not available on a charge of criminal damage because that is a basic-intent offence (see *DPP* v *Majewski*). However, for the offence of robbery (a crime of specific intent), Sam will be able to plead intoxication. We are told that he wandered unsteadily into the shop and that, after pushing Trisha, he collapsed in a drunken stupor. This shows that the *mens rea* for robbery may be negated, but that decision will be up to the jury to decide based on the facts.

(e) The defence of intoxication is well explained and the difference between specific- and basic-intent crimes clearly applied.

(e) **22–25/25 marks awarded. This is a sound answer. It clearly identifies the offence of theft. The question of whether or not Sam had any intention to permanently deprive could have been given a little more depth, as it may be argued that Sam did not have this intention initially, but in effect formed it later by damaging the shoes. The offence of making off without payment is well explained and applied. The element of force giving rise to a charge of robbery is correctly identified, and the case of *R* v *Hale* is rightly cited in a situation such as the present case where the robbery can be regarded as an ongoing act. The answer recognises that damage to the shoes reduces any hope the shop might have of ever selling them, and clearly identifies Sam's liability for criminal damage. The student's ability to explain the difference between basic- and specific-intent crimes in relation to the defence of intoxication shows good understanding.**

Section B

Question 1 **Pure economic loss**

An article in the IT pages of the *Herald*, a national newspaper, described and recommended Safestore, a security software package. After reading the article, Gordon bought a copy of Safestore and installed it on his computer's hard disk, hoping to protect his clients' confidential business information. In fact, the article had failed to explain that the version of Safestore on public sale was less comprehensive than the version reviewed. Gordon's security was breached 2 months later while he was online. In consequence, he had to pay a total of £30,000 to clients affected by the breach and he stopped receiving orders for his services. Gordon has now discovered that the manufacturer of Safestore has ceased to trade.

·Adapted from AQA examination paper, January 2004

Consider what rights Gordon may have against the *Herald* in connection with the £30,000 he had to pay out and his loss of business.

(25 marks)

e As with all such scenario 'problem-solving' questions, you are required to identify relevant legal issues, to define and explain relevant legal rules and then to apply these to provide (for a sound response) 'a sustainable analysis leading to satisfactory conclusions'. You need to use cases effectively to explain rules.

A-grade answer

As to whether Gordon has any rights against the *Herald* in respect of his £30,000 loss, it is necessary to consider the basic rules of the tort of negligence. The first major issue is whether or not in the circumstances the *Herald* owes Gordon a duty of care. The tests used to establish this are the 'neighbour' test from *Donoghue* v *Stevenson*, which relies on the question of foreseeability of harm or loss, and the more modern, incremental approach from *Caparo* v *Dickman*, which requires two further issues to be examined — proximity and policy.

It can certainly be argued that it was foreseeable that, as a result of the *Herald*'s negligently written article, a reader could suffer financial losses. However, the mere reading of a national newspaper is not by itself sufficient to establish proximity — closeness in terms of time, space or relationship. A further problem for Gordon is the policy test: whether it is just, fair and reasonable to impose a duty of care. This issue was considered in *Caparo*, where it was held by the House of Lords that a duty of care was not owed by the auditors to shareholders.

e This introduction affirms the basic rules of negligence effectively — economic loss is not a separate tort action. Too often students make the serious error of ignoring negligence rules, which form the basis of recovery of economic loss problems. Effective use is made of the *Caparo* rules, especially that of proximity.

The courts have decided that pure economic loss is not generally recoverable unless it is the direct result of injury to the claimant or damage to his or her property as in *Mulvaine* v *Joseph*, where a professional golfer was awarded an additional £1,000 for the loss of future prize money after he was injured in a road accident. Pure economic loss may also be recovered if it arises from a negligent misstatement made by the defendant to the claimant, provided there was a 'special relationship' between them when the misstatement was made. This rule was laid down in *Heller* v *Hedley Byrne*, where Lord Devlin defined the nature of the special relationship as 'a responsibility that is voluntarily undertaken, either generally where there is a general relationship such as that of solicitor and client, or specifically in relation to a particular transaction'.

Clearly, in this case, there can be no possibility of any general relationship between the *Herald* and one of its readers. As regards the specific circumstances referred to by Lord Devlin (that the party seeking information trusted the other to exercise such a degree of care as the circumstances required, that it was reasonable for him to do that, and that the other gave the information when he knew or ought to have known that the inquirer was relying on him), it is difficult to argue that these conditions existed here. While it is clear that the article was negligently written, the editor could hardly have known that any reader would rely on the advice given.

ⓔ The special relationship rules are stated and applied clearly.

This case can be distinguished from *De La Bere* v *Pearson*, where a newspaper's city editor offered individual financial advice to the claimant, who had written to him asking for the name of a reliable stockbroker. The editor replied suggesting a stockbroker who (unknown to him) was an undischarged bankrupt and who subsequently misappropriated the claimant's money. There, the editor was held to owe a duty of care because a special relationship existed. In the present case, the advice was given generally — not in response to a specific reader's request.

In *Smith* v *Bush*, liability was imposed on surveyors who negligently valued a house because the surveyors knew their survey report would be shown to prospective buyers and relied upon. It was held that the surveyors had 'assumed responsibility' to them. In the present case, there would appear to be no grounds for asserting the newspaper had assumed any responsibility to Gordon. Finally, in *James McNaughton Paper Groups* v *Hicks Anderson*, where the defendant accountants became aware that the claimants were considering a takeover of their clients, it was held that no duty of care was owed. The draft accounts, which they had been asked to confirm in general terms to the claimants, had not been prepared for their benefit and the defendants would reasonably expect a party to a takeover bid to take independent advice and not rely exclusively on these draft accounts.

A similar argument could be advanced on behalf of the *Herald* newspaper. The editor could not reasonably expect any reader, far less a professional businessman, to rely exclusively on that article and buy the security software package without taking further steps to ensure that Safestore could be installed to protect his clients' confidential business information. In conclusion, Gordon would appear to have no rights against the *Herald*.

ⓔ **24–25/25 marks awarded. In terms of both explaining legal rules and applying them, this is a successful answer. The answer gives a full explanation of the general rules governing pure economic loss and the particular rules concerning negligent misstatements, with *Hedley Byrne* being fully explained. There is also a sound application of this rule to the facts, which is considerably strengthened by the distinction drawn between the facts in *De La Bere* and the present scenario.**

The reference to these additional cases confirms the student's sound grasp of the key rules of economic loss arising from negligent misstatement, and provides the basis of a well-reasoned application and conclusion. Above all, this answer demonstrates how thoroughly students need to understand the facts of key cases and then how to use these to provide a strong argument and conclusion.

Question 2 Occupier's duty to lawful and unlawful visitors

Gordon engaged Ian to repair damage to a wall in his house. While doing so, Ian cut through an electricity cable and fused the power supply. Gordon was out, so Ian opened the locked door to the cellar with a key hanging from a nail on a nearby wall. As he went down the cellar stairs to find the electricity unit, a rotten stair gave way under his weight and he fell, breaking his leg and ripping his clothes.

Adapted from AQA examination paper, January 2004

Consider what rights Ian may have against Gordon in connection with his broken leg and his ripped clothes.

(25 marks)

ⓔ As with all such scenario 'problem-solving' questions, you are required to identify relevant legal issues, to define and explain relevant legal rules and then to apply these to provide (for a sound response) 'a sustainable analysis leading to satisfactory conclusions'. You need to use cases effectively to explain rules.

A-grade answer

The issue of what rights Ian may have against Gordon depends largely on whether Ian was a lawful visitor or a trespasser at the time when he opened the cellar door and fell through the rotten stairs. The law dealing with an occupier's liability towards lawful visitors is the Occupiers' Liability Act 1957, which codified the common law duty of care. Section 2 describes this as a duty to take such care as is reasonable in the circumstances to see that the visitor will be reasonably safe in using the premises for the purposes for which he or she is invited or permitted to be there. Clearly, Ian is a lawful visitor in respect of the repair to Gordon's wall, and Gordon is the occupier, as it is his house, and Gordon has a sufficient degree of control over it as stipulated by Lord Denning MR in *Wheat* v *Lacon*.

ⓔ This is a strong introduction which clearly explains the important issues of both occupier and lawful visitor.

As Ian is presumably an expert tradesman — probably a builder — the appropriate section to be considered is s.2(3)(b) of the 1957 Act. This states that an occupier who invites tradesmen to enter his or her premises to carry out their ordinary work is entitled to assume that they are aware of any special risks associated with that work and that they will take precautions accordingly. The leading case is that of *Roles* v *Nathan*, where the Court of Appeal held that the warning given by the occupier to chimney sweeps had been adequate, given that the sweeps were exercising their profession and should already have been aware of the dangers.

In the present case, it is at least questionable whether cutting through an electricity cable could be regarded as a special risk associated with the task of repairing a wall. There is no indication that Gordon warned Ian about the presence of an electricity cable. If the cable ran through the wall in an unusual direction, it could be argued that Gordon breached his common law duty to Ian by failing to warn him. Furthermore, it is doubtful that a rotten staircase to a basement would be regarded as a risk incidental to plastering a wall. Lord Denning MR envisaged this very scenario in *Roles* v *Nathan*, when he stated that the defendants would not have been liable if the stairs leading to the basement had given way, as this was not a risk ordinarily incidental to the work of a chimney sweep. If the risk is not incidental to the work of the expert visitor, the law is clear: the fact that the visitor is an expert will not of itself free the occupier from liability if the expert is injured as a foreseeable consequence of negligence by the occupier. This was the position in *Ogwo* v *Taylor*, decided on the basis of common law negligence, where the householder who started a fire by his careless use of a blowlamp was liable for injuries suffered by a fireman in fighting the blaze.

ⓔ These paragraphs effectively demonstrate how to explain relevant rules through the use of leading cases. The application of these rules is then developed well.

The power supply having been fused, it would be foreseeable that, in Gordon's absence, a tradesman would try to carry out the relatively straightforward task of replacing the fuse by locating the fuse box. There was no notice warning anyone not to enter the cellar. Indeed, the proximity of the key strengthens Ian's case to be a lawful visitor. On the simple principle of the neighbour test in *Donoghue* v *Stevenson*, it would not be difficult to establish that Gordon owed Ian a duty of care, which he breached and which was the cause of Ian's injury and his ripped clothes. Ian would therefore be able to claim damages for both the injury and the cost of replacing those clothes.

However, it is necessary to consider the other possible position: that Ian, although initially a lawful visitor, became a trespasser as soon as he entered the cellar. If the visitor ceases to use the premises for the purpose for which he or she is invited to be there, then no duty is owed under the 1957 Act. As Scrutton LJ stated in *The Calgarth* (1927): 'When you invite a person into your house to use the stairs, you do not invite him to slide down the banisters.' Before the case of *Herrington* v *British Rail Board*, no duty of care was owed to trespassers. The decision in that case was incorporated in the Occupiers' Liability Act 1984, which imposed a duty to trespassers in the following circumstances: where the occupier is aware of the danger or has reasonable grounds to believe that it exists (s.1(3)(a)); where the occupier knows or has reasonable grounds to believe that the trespasser is in the vicinity of the danger or that he or she may come into the vicinity of the danger (s.1(3)(b)); and where the risk is one against which, in all the circumstances of the case, the occupier may reasonably be expected to offer the trespasser some protection (s.1(3)(c)).

ⓔ For a 'sound' response, alternative solutions often need to be considered as they are here.

It could be argued that Gordon was aware of the rotten state of the cellar staircase because, if the main electricity supply of his house came into his cellar, he may have entered the cellar occasionally to check the meter reading, if for no other reason. The second test could also be met because the fact that the key to the cellar was hanging from a nail on a nearby wall is suggestive of the likelihood of someone entering the cellar. The final requirement — that the risk is one against which Gordon may be expected to offer Ian some protection — is surely also satisfied. At the very least, the key should not have been so readily available or Gordon should have placed a warning notice on the door or given Ian a specific warning against entering the cellar. However, although it can be argued Gordon was liable under the 1984 Act for Ian's broken leg, he would not be liable for the damage to Ian's clothing because s.1(8) provides that trespassers are not entitled to sue in respect of property damage.

ⓔ Note how each of the key rules that determine the circumstances in which a duty is owed to trespassers is first explained and then applied. Too often, students merely list the rules without attempting to consider their application in the specific circumstances of the scenario.

ⓔ **25/25 marks awarded. The answer is sound on both explanation and application and deals capably with both elements — duties to lawful visitors and trespassers.**

Question 3 **Damages for psychiatric injury**

Javed owned a warehouse with an open yard surrounded by a low wall. For years, the yard was little used and members of the public treated it as a short cut from a main road to a housing estate. Then Javed began to store materials in the yard and put up a light fencing and signs warning that the yard was private property. Recently, the signs have been torn down, gaps in the fencing have appeared and members of the public, including Ken, have been using the yard as a short cut again. Ken was crossing the yard while Les, an inexperienced forklift truck driver, was trying to stack heavy crates. As Ken tried to slip through a narrow gap, the stack of crates toppled over and he was crushed and badly injured.

Mike had been assisting Les and had narrowly avoided being crushed himself. He immediately got down on the ground and tried to assist Ken. The incident was witnessed by Mike's sister, Nicola, who had come to collect him from work. She could just glimpse

Mike's legs and thought that he had been crushed in the incident. She immediately became hysterical and was taken away for treatment. Mike found it difficult to recover from the experience and was off work for weeks. Nicola suffered panic attacks for the next few months.

Adapted from AQA examination paper, January 2003

Consider what rights Mike and Nicola may have against Javed.

(25 marks)

ⓔ As with all such scenario 'problem-solving' questions, you are required to identify relevant legal issues, to define and explain relevant legal rules and then to apply these to provide (for a sound response) 'a sustainable analysis leading to satisfactory conclusions'. You need to use cases effectively to explain rules.

A-grade answer

With regard to both potential claimants — Mike and Nicola — it is necessary to examine the relevant issues concerning recovery of damages for psychiatric injury.

There are two key questions to be addressed in all such claims. The first deals with the basic principles of the tort of negligence — whether the claimant was owed a duty of care by the defendant, whether in the circumstances of the case the defendant breached that duty, and finally whether the injury was caused by the breach and was not too remote. The second issue is whether the claimant was a primary or secondary victim.

As a fellow employee, Mike was owed a duty of care by his employer under both occupier's liability and the neighbour principle of foreseeable injury or loss (*Donoghue* v *Stevenson*), and it seems clear that Les, an inexperienced forklift truck driver, breached that duty of care when the stack of crates toppled over. The 'reasonable forklift driver' would not have caused the crates to topple, and under the test laid down in *Nettleship* v *Weston*, the test is objective and does not take into account Les's inexperience. The consequence of Mike's difficulties, which caused him to be off work for weeks, was not too remote from the breach (the *Wagon Mound* test) and, if the injuries had been physical rather than psychiatric, Mike would have had no difficulty in recovering damages. Mike has, however, found it hard to recover from the experience, and this suggests nervous shock. The legal rule is that there must be some recognisable psychiatric injury, supported by medical evidence. Ordinary human emotions such as grief and distress do not qualify as nervous shock. In *Reilly* v *Merseyside Health Authority*, the claimants could not recover damages for their panic when they were trapped in a lift for over an hour.

ⓔ Although this question deals with psychiatric injury, the basic rules of negligence still need to be dealt with, and the student covers all three rules effectively — duty, breach and remoteness. Of particular interest is the reference to *Nettleship* in connection with breach of duty, addressing the fact that Les was an inexperienced driver. Students need to be able to identify relevant cases from the facts of the scenario.

The fact that Mike was off work for weeks could indicate that he was suffering from a diagnosable psychiatric injury. If that is indeed the case, the next issue is whether Mike is a primary or secondary victim. Primary victims are those directly affected by the negligent act, those who believe themselves to be in physical danger, and rescuers — provided they believed that they were in danger of physical injury. In the circumstances, it could be argued that Mike was a primary victim, in respect of his being a rescuer (*Chadwick* v *British Transport Commission*), and also of his being in the immediate vicinity of the accident and thus in fear about his own safety. He 'narrowly avoided being crushed himself' and so comes within the test established in *Dulieu* v *White*. The case of *Chadwick* established the general rule that rescuers will be treated as primary victims, provided they can show close involvement with the incident (which Mike would have no difficulty proving). The House of Lords in *White* v *Chief Constable of South Yorkshire* introduced the requirement for rescuers to have placed themselves in danger, or perceived that they were doing so, when making a claim in respect of psychiatric injury. Primary victims can claim for psychiatric injury under the normal rules of negligence, therefore Mike should be able to claim damages to compensate him for his weeks off work.

(e) The issue of whether the claimant is a primary or secondary victim is crucial in such questions. All the various factors need to be identified and explained properly. This has been done well here, with relevant cases used to provide a sound foundation to both argument and conclusion. Note how clearly the issue of 'rescuers' is explained and applied.

Nicola's position is more problematic. She is not a primary victim under any of the categories explained above. She would have to establish that the defendant was in breach of his duty of care towards her, and that his negligence caused her psychiatric injuries. It could be argued that Javed owed her a duty of care, arising both from occupier's liability (Occupiers' Liability Act 1957) and the 'neighbour' principle referred to above. The law governing the right of secondary victims to claim for nervous shock has been clearly laid down by the House of Lords in *Alcock* v *Chief Constable of South Yorkshire*. To make a successful claim, a secondary victim has to be present at the shocking event itself or its immediate aftermath, must have close ties of love and affection with the primary victim, and must have learned of the event by his or her own unaided senses. Finally, the psychiatric injury must be induced by the sudden appreciation of the horrifying event, rather than gradually developing over a period of time.

Nicola could argue that that she satisfies at least three of these requirements. She was present at the incident and witnessed it herself, and the psychiatric injury was induced suddenly. Furthermore, it would appear that Nicola has suffered a recognisable psychiatric injury because she received treatment. There could be some difficulty with the requirement that there should be close ties of love and affection with the primary victim. In *Alcock* this was restricted in general to spouses and parent/child relationships, although it was suggested in *obiter dicta* that siblings might also be able to recover damages if they could produce sufficient evidence of such ties of love and affection.

ⓔ The issue of Nicola being a secondary victim is explained comprehensively. *Alcock* is the key case for this, and a sound answer requires all three tests to be addressed, as has been done here. The reference to the *obiter* statement (on the question of siblings) is useful in confirming the depth of the student's understanding of this particular rule.

In conclusion, it can be argued that Mike would be entitled to recover damages for his time off work as a primary victim, and that Nicola, provided she can satisfy the test of close love and affection, would be able to recover damages as a secondary victim.

ⓔ **25/25 marks awarded. Overall, this answer is sound on negligence rules and on primary and secondary victims; all key cases are well used and there is sound application.**

Question 4 Nuisance and *Rylands* v *Fletcher*

Residents living in the vicinity of the Johnsons factory had been complaining for some time of the noise and vibration coming from the factory, especially at night. When an explosion occurred in the factory one morning, a thick cloud of smoke spread rapidly across the town, leaving a dirty, oily deposit on houses and other buildings.

Adapted from AQA examination paper, January 2004

Consider what rights and indicate what remedies residents of the houses affected by the noise, vibration and explosion may have against Johnsons.

(25 marks)

ⓔ As with all such scenario 'problem-solving' questions, you are required to identify relevant legal issues, to define and explain relevant legal rules and then to apply these to provide (for a sound response) 'a sustainable analysis leading to satisfactory conclusions'. You need to use cases effectively to explain rules.

A-grade answer

The tort of private nuisance is concerned with the protection of interests in land and the restrictions imposed on an occupier so that an occupier of adjacent land is not unreasonably disturbed. The tort is ill defined, but is best described as a substantial and unreasonable interference with the claimant's land or with his or her enjoyment of it. Different types of damage can amount to a private nuisance: physical damage to the claimant's property, loss of value to the claimant's property (although this is somewhat uncertain), and interference with the claimant's enjoyment of his or her property. Examples include excessive noise (*Christie* v *Davey*) or causing dust or noxious smells.

ⓔ This is a sound introduction to the tort of private nuisance.

To bring an action in private nuisance, a claimant must normally be a person with a legal or equitable interest in the land affected. A mere relative or visitor has no cause of action. This principle was seen in the case of *Malone* v *Laskey* and affirmed by the House of Lords in *Hunter* v *Canary Wharf*. The whole law of private nuisance is a matter of balancing competing interests — the occupier's right to use his or her land as he or she wishes against the neighbour's right to enjoy his or her land — and depends on questions of reasonableness. As to the duration of the nuisance, it is a general rule that the courts will not grant relief against a nuisance unless the interference is of substantial duration.

In the present scenario, it is obvious that the people complaining are the occupiers of the houses or have a legal interest in them. Assuming they were the owners of the factory, Johnsons would be held liable. Even if they leased the factory from the owners, they would still be held liable for its activities because of the control they exercised over operating times. It can be argued that the nuisance must have been occurring for a substantial period, as the residents have been complaining for 'some time'. It is also clear that because there are a number of residents who have complained, the locality is not exclusively an industrial one which the court will take into consideration. This may mean that the courts could grant relief.

ⓔ The key elements of nuisance are clearly explained and applied — claimants having legal interest, defendants having control over the factory, and locality and duration.

The remedies that may be available include damages or an injunction to restrain the continuation of the nuisance. An injunction is usually the preferred remedy for the claimant, as it requires the defendant to stop the nuisance. It can also be tailored to meet the exact circumstances of the case and produce a just solution. In this case, the residents may be awarded damages, but it is more likely that the court would grant them an injunction. This might mean that the Johnsons factory could operate only during certain hours and would have to stop operations at a certain time at night. Another remedy, which the defendants would no doubt prefer, would be a court order requiring them to install better sound insulation, which would enable them to continue operating during the night without causing as much disturbance.

ⓔ This is an effective — and imaginative — paragraph in which sensible injunctions are suggested.

The noise, vibration — and especially the explosion — could also be classed as a public nuisance. A public nuisance (which is a crime as well as a tort) is an act or omission not warranted by law, which affects the comfort and convenience of a group of people. The harm does not have to be something that only affects the land; it can be damage to goods or financial loss. The facts in this case are similar to that of *Attorney General* v *PYA Quarries*, where residents living near a quarry were disturbed by vibrations from an explosion and by dust. At the request of local authorities, the Attorney General successfully sought an injunction restraining the quarry owners from conducting their work so as to occasion the nuisance by dust or by vibration.

(e) This is a brief explanation of public nuisance which would often be omitted from such an answer.

The tort of *Rylands* v *Fletcher* has its origins in the law of nuisance but has developed as a separate tort with its own rules. It imposes liability for the escape from land of something that causes damage. The tort was defined by Blackburn J in *Rylands* v *Fletcher*. He said that a person who, for his or her own purposes, brings onto his or her land and collects and keeps there anything likely to do mischief if it escapes, must keep it at his or her peril and, if he or she does not do so, then he or she is answerable for all the damage that is the natural consequence of the escape. Lord Cairns in the House of Lords drew a distinction between what he described as 'natural use', such as the natural accumulation of rainwater, and 'non-natural use', such as the storage of water in a purpose-built reservoir. In the case of a natural use, there would be no liability for damage caused by its escape. In *Rylands* v *Fletcher*, the defendant had employed an independent contractor to build a reservoir on his land. Through the contractor's negligence, water escaped through some old mine workings and flooded current workings on the claimant's land. It was held that the claimant was entitled to damages. With the rule in *Rylands* v *Fletcher*, the thing accumulated need not be dangerous in itself, but must be likely to cause damage if it escapes. For the defendant to be liable, the thing will have to have moved from the defendant's land to cause damage elsewhere. If there is no escape, there can be no liability. There is some flexibility, so a fire or the blast of an explosion will probably be treated as a 'dangerous substance'.

The case of *Read* v *Lyons* can be distinguished from the present case, as there the claimant was injured in the explosion and the claim failed as no escape occurred. The rule in *Rylands* v *Fletcher* applies only to 'non-natural' use of the land — i.e. to some extraordinary and unusual use — and only where the thing that escapes is likely to cause danger. In the present case it is clear that the factory was not a natural use of the land and as a result, there was an escape of dust leaving dirty, oily deposits on houses and other buildings. This dust would be defined as a dangerous thing, as it was likely to cause damage and did cause damage. Johnsons would, therefore, be liable for the dirt on the buildings, as it was caused by an escape.

(e) All the rules of *Rylands* v *Fletcher* are clearly explained and then applied.

As to the remedies that may be available with reference to the explosion, general damages would be most suitable. An injunction would not be appropriate, as it is not a regular occurrence. Any damages awarded would be to compensate for the damage done to the buildings.

(e) **24 or 25/25 marks awarded.**

Knowledge check answers

1 The case of *R* v *Lawrence* clarified this. Although the Italian student had consented to the taking of the money, it was consent for a specific amount — not consent to take more. This is backed up by *R* v *Gomez* and also *R* v *Hinks*.

2 *Oxford* v *Moss* tells us that 'knowledge' cannot be stolen as it is not property under s.2.

3 *Attorney General's Reference (No. 1)* (1983). In this case an employer was paid more salary than the employee was entitled to. It was held that the employee was legally obliged to return it.

4 Where the defendant believes he or she has the right in law to take the item; where he or she has taken reasonable steps to find the owner; where he or she believes the owner of the property would consent to the appropriation.

5 Conditional intent is where the defendant's intention to permanently deprive is based on a condition. The leading case is *R* v *Easom* (1971) in which the defendant picked up a woman's handbag in a cinema, looked inside it and then replaced it without taking anything. He was not guilty of theft.

6 A completed theft must be proven — so as long as all elements of theft can be proven, and force was used, then robbery would succeed.

7 *R* v *Dawson and James*.

8 If the theft is deemed to be a continuing act, the force can be used at any point during this continuing act.

9 The defendant must have the necessary *mens rea* for the completed theft — dishonesty (s. 2) and the intention to permanently deprive (s.6), as well as intending to use the force or threat of force in order to steal from the victim.

10 The key difference is the intention of the defendant. S.9(1)(a) is when the intention to commit an ulterior offence is formed before entering the building as a trespasser. In s.9(1)(b) the defendant enters the building as a trespasser and then forms the intention to commit an ulterior offence.

11 Entry can be 'substantial and effective' (*R* v *Collins*) or 'effective' only (*R* v *Brown* and *R* v *Ryan*).

12 *R* v *Walkington* shows us that a defendant would be deemed a trespasser if he or she enters a building with permission but then goes into part of the same building where the permission has not been given. In this case, Walkington went behind a shop counter.

13 A trespasser is someone who does not have permission to be there. If you do have permission you are not a trespasser unless you go beyond the permission that was originally given, e.g. *R* v *Jones*.

14 The defendant must know or be reckless as to trespassing — and the defendant must have the appropriate *mens rea* for the ulterior offences under either 9(1)(a) or 9(1)(b).

15 It must first be shown that payment was required for the goods or services and then the defendant must make off — he or she must completely leave the premises.

16 There was not enough evidence to show that the defendant intended to avoid payment altogether — he claimed that he genuinely hoped to be able to pay at a later stage.

17 If the item of property will require time, money and effort to restore it to its original state then this will be deemed damage, as in the case of *Roe* v *Kingerlee* (1986).

18 The *Cunningham* test must be applied — the defendant must have thought about the possible risk that his or her actions could have caused criminal damage but gone ahead with his or her actions anyway. This is referred to as taking an unjustified risk.

19 Lawful excuse is found under section 5: s.5(2)(a) is where the defendant believes the owner would have consented to the damage and s.5(2)(b) is where the defendant believes the property was in immediate need of protection.

20 Basic criminal damage under s.1(1) allows the defendant to raise lawful excuse under section 5. This is not available for s.1(2).

21 Express is where the defendant actually says something that is untrue or misleading and implied is simply an action that is untrue or misleading.

22 You must apply the *R* v *Ghosh* test — this has both objective and subjective elements. Would a reasonable person deem the defendant's actions as dishonest and did the defendant realise his or her actions would be dishonest by those standards?

23 Section 11 of the Fraud Act 2006 is obtaining services dishonestly — the defendant must obtain any service in a dishonest way, knowing that he or she will not pay for the service. Section 3 of the Theft Act 1978 is making off without payment. The goods/service are obtained in an honest way, but the defendant has made off without paying.

24 The defendant must be dishonest as to obtaining the service — the *R* v *Ghosh* test must be applied. Also the defendant must intend to avoid payment in full or in part for the service that has been provided.

25 Under s.21(1)(a) if the defendant has the belief that he or she has reasonable grounds to make the demand and s.21(1)(b) if the defendant has the belief that the use of the menace is a proper means of reinforcing the demand.

26 If the duress is self-induced the defence will become weak. Self-induced is where the person threatening the defendant is known to the defendant for his or her violent nature, or the defendant could have been a member of a violent gang — this is referred to as prior known association.

27 Basic-intent crimes are those that require the lesser form of *mens rea* — recklessness. Specific-intent crimes require intention only.

28 Involuntary intoxication — following the rules of *Majewski* — can be raised to both basic- and specific-intent crimes, but the defence will only succeed if the *mens rea* is fully negated.

29 When the defendant is either defending him/herself, or another, or preventing a crime.

30 Because it was not proved that the manufacturers had actually caused the fault.

31 The manufacturer of the actual product and also the manufacturer of a component; any person who brand-names a product or by other means holds himself or herself out to be the producer; the importer of a product into the EU.

32 Section 3 defines a defect as existing when 'the safety of the product is not such as persons generally are entitled to expect'.

33 *Wilsher v Essex Area Health Authority.*

34 That provided it could be proved that the doctor's negligence had *materially increased* the risk of injury, the defendant could be held liable.

35 It must be a recognised psychiatric illness which occurred as a result of the accident and has long-term effects.

36 *Dulieu v White and Sons.*

37 That the primary victim does not need to show that psychiatric injury was foreseeable, merely that some kind of personal injury was foreseeable, and that the primary victim does not need to be a person of normal fortitude.

38 Because of the potentially endless liability that could attach to the defendant — the 'floodgates' argument.

39 The three key control tests are:
- The secondary victim must have close ties of love and affection with the primary victim.
- The psychiatric injury must be caused through the victim's own, unaided sight and hearing of an event or its immediate aftermath.
- The psychiatric injury must be induced by shock.

40 To recover compensation for psychiatric injury, rescuers must objectively have placed themselves in danger, or reasonably have perceived themselves to be doing so.

41 Because it was an insurance company which had no special skill in giving investment advice.

42 Because he had not relied on the advice as he had bought the company to obtain the services of its directors.

43 That the liability of the solicitor to the would-be beneficiary was based on the neighbour test, and that where a solicitor is instructed to carry out a transaction for the benefit of a third party, that party is clearly within contemplation as being likely to be affected — the fact that the loss is purely financial should be no bar to a claim.

44 Someone who is present on the premises by the occupier's invitation, or with the occupier's express or implied permission, or in exercise of a legal right.

45 Because what may pose no threat to an adult may nevertheless be dangerous to a child.

46 Because the occupier who had negligently set fire to his house owed a duty to rescuers.

47 The occupier's liability is discharged if the occupier gives effective warning of the danger provided the warning is sufficient to enable the visitor to be reasonably safe.

48 Because it had not taken reasonable care to select competent contractors — the key issue was that it had not insisted that the independent contractor take out public-liability insurance.

49 A duty is owed by a person as occupier of premises to persons other than visitors in respect of any risk of their suffering injury on the premises *by reason of any danger due to the state of the premises.*

50 Section 1(3)(b): the occupier knows or has reasonable grounds to believe that the other is in the vicinity of the danger concerned or that he may come into the vicinity of the danger.

51 *St Helens Smelting Co. v Tipping.*

52 Because the paper which was damaged was unusually sensitive whereas ordinary paper would not have been affected by the rise in temperature.

53 A partial injunction limiting both the number of days on which racing could take place and the number and power of the boats allowed to take part.

54 That for an individual to sue under public nuisance, he or she has to show special damage. Also, that damages for personal injury are recoverable in public nuisance.

55 Because the harmful effects of their businesses were inevitable, and an injunction would have defeated the original legislative intention.

56 *Cambridge Water Co. Ltd v Eastern Counties Leather plc.*

57 *Cambridge Water Co. Ltd v Eastern Counties Leather plc.*

58 That in cases involving a 'loaned employee', both employers should be vicariously liable if both had some control over his or her actions.

59 Because he was still carrying out what he was employed to do — deliver milk.

60 He had identified himself to the claimant as a police officer and had acted as one, albeit badly.

61 That the key question was 'what was the cause of the damage'; *not* 'what was the cause of the accident'.

62 A person cannot use *volenti* as a defence if he/she has no knowledge of the risk — even if objectively the reasonable person would have been aware of the risk.

63 Because the claimant had knowingly and willingly gone on a flight with a drunken pilot.

Index